Over 450 Recession Busting Healthy Crockpot recipes!

Money-Wise Ted Wilcox

Over 450 Recession Busting Healthy Crockpot recipes!

Copyright © 2009 by Money-Wise Ted Wilcox

FearlessPublishing.Net

Let's save money!

16 BEAN SOUP
    1 package 16 Bean Soup
    3 bay leaves
    1 tablespoon crushed oregano
    2 cans no-fat chicken stock
    Additional water to cover
    3 stalks celery chopped
    3 carrots diced
    1 large onion chopped
    3 cloves garlic sliced
    1 pound turkey Italian sausage sliced
    2 cans stewed (or diced) tomatoes

Combine first 5 ingredients (liquid should cover mixture by 1"-2") in Crock Pot Cook on high for 2 hours Add remaining ingredients and shift cooker to low and cook for additional 3 hours For more zing, add cayenne or crushed red pepper when adding second set of ingredients. Serve as complete meal or over rice. Freezes well.

ALL DAY CROCKPOT DELIGHT
    2-3 lbs. boneless chuck, cut into 1 inch cubes
    1/2 c. flour
    1/4 c. butter
    1 onion, sliced
    1 tsp. salt
    1/8 tsp. pepper
    1 clove garlic, minced
    2 c. beer
    1/4 c. flour

Coat beef cubes with the 1/2 cup flour. Brown in melted butter. Drain off excess fat. In crock pot, combine browned meat with onion, salt, pepper, garlic and beer.

Cover and cook on low 5-7 hours (all day) until meat is tender. Turn control to high. Dissolve remaining 1/4 cup flour in small amount of water. Stir into meat mixture, cook on high 30-40 minutes. Serve with rice and salad.

ALL DAY MACARONI AND CHEESE
8 ounces elbow macaroni, cooked and drained
4 cups(16 ounces) shredded sharp Chedder Cheese
1 can (12 ounces) evaporated milk
1 1/2 cups milk
2 eggs
1 teaspoon salt
1/2 teaspoon black pepper

Place the cooked macaroni in crockpot that has been sprayed with nonstick cooking spray. Add the remaining ingredients, all except 1 cup of the cheese, mix well.

Sprinkle with the remaining 1 cup of cheese and then cover and cook on low setting for 5 to 6 hours or until the mixture is firm and golden around the edges. Do not remove the cover or stir until it has finished cooking.

APPLE BROWN BETTY
* 3 lbs. cooking apples
* 10 slices of bread, cubed (about 4 cups)
* 1/2 tsp. cinnamon
* 1/4 tsp. nutmeg
* 1/8 tsp. salt
* 3/4 c. brown sugar
* 1/2 c. butter or margarine, melted

Wash apples, peel, core, cut into eighths; place in bottom on crock. Combine bread cubes, cinnamon, nutmeg, salt, sugar, butter; toss together. Place on top of apples in crock. Cover. Place crock into outer shell. Cook on low setting 2 to 4 hours.

Makes 6 to 8 servings.

APPLE BUTTER
This can be made in a slow cooker/Crock Pot or oven at 325 degrees for 3-4 hours.

4 qts. unsweetened applesauce
7 C. granulated sugar
1-1/3 C. brown sugar
5-1/3 T. cider vinegar
5-1/3 T. lemon juice
2 teaspoon. cinnamon

2 teaspoon. allspice

1 teaspoon. ground cloves

Combine all ingredients in a slow cooker/Crock Pot or roasting pan. Cover and cook 3 hours, stirring occasionally. Remove lid and continue cooking until excess liquid cooks away (turn to low as necessary) Slow Cooker 5-8 hours, oven 3-5 hours Seal mixture in hot jars and process in a hot water bath for 10 minutes.

Makes approximately 8-10 pints

APPLE-COCONUT CRISP

4 large Granny Smith apples, peeled & coarsely sliced (about 4 cups)

1/2 cup sweetened flaked coconut

1 tablespoon flour

1/3 cup brown sugar

1/2 cup butterscotch or caramel ice cream topping (fat-free is fine)

1/2 teaspoon cinnamon

1/3 cup flour

1/2 cup quick rolled oats

2 tablespoons butter or margarine

In a casserole 1 1/2-quart baking dish that fits in the slow cooker/Crock Pot, combine apples with coconut, 1 tablespoon flour, 1/3 cup brown sugar, and cinnamon. Drizzle with the ice cream topping. Combine remaining ingredients in a small bowl with a fork or pastry cutter and sprinkle over apple mixture. Cover and cook on high for 2 1/2 to 3 hours, until apples are tender. Serve warm with vanilla ice cream or whipped topping.

APPLE CRANBERRY COMPOTE

6 cooking apples, peeled, slice

1 cup fresh cranberries

1 cup sugar

1/2 teaspoons grated orange peel

1/2 cups water

1/4 cups port wine

sour cream , (low fat)

Arrange apple slices and cranberries in slow cooker/Crock Pot. Sprinkle sugar over fruit. Add orange peel, water and wine. Stir to mix

ingredients. Cover, cook on low 4-6 hours, until apples are tender. Serve warm fruits with the juices, topped with a dab of sour cream.
    Serves 6.

APPLE CRANBERRY CRISP
    * 3 apples (Any kind - I personally like Gala)
    * 1 cup cranberries
    * 3/4 cup brown sugar
    * 1/3 cup rolled oats (quick cooking)
    * 1/4 tsp. salt
    * 1 tsp. cinnamon
    * 1/3 cup butter, softened

Peel, core and slice apples. Place apple slices and cranberries in cp. Mix remaining ingredients in separate bowl and sprinkle over top of apple and cranberries. Place 4 or 5 paper towels over the top of the crockpot, place an object (I use a wooden spoon) across the top of the crockpot and set lid on top. This allows the steam to escape. Turn crockpot on high and cook for about 2 hours.
    Serves 4.

APPLE DATE PUDDING
    * 4-5 apples, peeled, cored and diced
    * 3/4 cup sugar, or less, to taste
    * 1/2 cup chopped dates
    * 1/2 cup toasted, chopped pecans
    * 2 tbs. flour
    * 1 tsp. baking powder
    * 1/8 tsp. salt
    * 1/4 tsp. nutmeg
    * 2 tbs. melted butter
    * 1 egg, beaten

In the slow cooker, place apples, sugar, dates and pecans; stir. In a separate bowl, mix together flour, baking powder, salt and nutmeg and stir into apple mixture. Drizzle melted butter over batter and stir. Stir in egg. Set cooker on low and cook for 3 to 4 hours. Serve warm.
    NOTE: If crispier nuts are desired, add toasted pecans at the end of cooking period.

APPLE GLAZED PORK ROAST
4 lb. pork loin roast
6 apples
1/4 cup apple juice
3 T. brown sugar
1 t. ginger, ground

Rub roast with salt and pepper. Brown pork roast under broiler to remove excess fat; drain well. Core and quarter apples. Place apple quarters in bottom of crockpot. Place roast on top of apples. Combine apple juice, brown sugar, and ginger. Spoon over top surface of roast, moistening well. Cover and cook on Low for 10-12 hours, until done.

APPLE-NUT CHEESECAKE
Crust:
1 cup (scant) graham cracker crumbs
1/2 teaspoon cinnamon
2 tablespoons sugar
3 tablespoons butter, melted
1/4 cup finely chopped pecans or walnuts
Filling:
16 ounces cream cheese
1/4 cup brown sugar
1/2 cup granulated white sugar
2 large eggs
3 tablespoons heavy whipping cream
1 tablespoon cornstarch
1 teaspoon vanilla
Topping:
1 large apple, thinly sliced (about 1 1/2 cups)
1 teaspoon cinnamon
1/4 cup sugar
1 tablespoon finely chopped pecans or walnuts

Combine crust ingredients; pat into a 7-inch springform pan.

Beat sugars into cream cheese until smooth and creamy. Beat in eggs, whipping cream, cornstarch, and vanilla. Beat for about 3 minutes on medium speed of a hand-held electric mixer. Pour mixture into the prepared crust. Combine apple slices with sugar, cinnamon and nuts; place topping evenly over the top of cheesecake. Place the cheesecake on a rack (or "ring" of aluminum foil to keep it off the bottom of the pot) in the Crock Pot. Cover and cook on high for 2 1/2 to 3 hours. Let stand in the covered pot (after turning it off) for about 1 to 2 hours, until cool enough to handle. Cool thoroughly before removing pan sides. Chill before serving; store leftovers in the refrigerator.

APPLE PIE COFFEE CAKE

Apple Mixture:

1 can (20 oz) apple pie filling, apple slices broken up somewhat

1/2 teaspoon cinnamon

3 tablespoons brown sugar

Cake Batter:

2 small yellow cake mixes (Jiffy - 9-ounce each)

2 eggs, beaten

1/2 cup sour cream (light)

3 tablespoons softened butter or margarine

1/2 cup evaporated milk

1/2 teaspoon cinnamon

1 teaspoon butter or margarine for greasing slow cooker/Crock Pot

Combine ingredients for apple mixture in a small bowl. Combine batter ingredients; mix well.

Generouslly butter the sides and bottom of a 3 1/2 quart slow cooker/Crock Pot. Spread about half the apple mixture in the bottom of the pot. Spoon 1/2 the batter over the apple mixture. Spoon the remaining apple mixture over the batter, then cover with remaining batter. Cover and cook on high for 2 to 2 1/2 hours. Turn heat off, leave cover ajar slightly, and cool for about 15 minutes. Invert on a plate, retrieving any apples left in the bottom of the pot and placing on top of the cake. Makes a cake about 7 inches in diameter and 3 1/2-inches high.

APPLE PUDDING CAKE

* 2 cups sugar
* 1 cup vegetable oil
* 2 eggs
* 2 teaspoons vanilla
* 2 cups flour

* 1 teaspoon baking soda
* 1 teaspoon nutmeg
* 2 cups unpeeled apple, finely chopped
* 1 cup chopped nuts (walnuts or pecans)

Beat sugar, oil, eggs, and vanilla. Add apple with dry ingredients and mix well. Spray a two pound tin can with cooking spray or grease and flour it well. Pour batter into can, filling no more than 2/3 full. Place can in Crock Pot. Do not add water. Cover but leave cover ajar so steam can escape. Cook on high 3 1/2 to 4 hours. Don't peek before the last hour of baking. Cake is done when top is set. Let stand in can a few minutes before tipping pudding out on a plate. Serve half-rounds plain, with whipped topping, or a pudding sauce.

APPLESAUCE SAUERKRAUT

4 cups sauerkraut, rinsed and drained
2 cups sweetened applesauce
1/2 tsp caraway seeds
1 tbs butter or margarine

Combine all ingredients. Place in a greased 2 quart casserole. Bake at 375° F. for 30 to 45 minutes.

Serves 6.

APRICOT NUT BREAD

* 3/4 cup dried apricots
* 1 cup flour
* 2 tsp baking powder
* 1/4 tsp baking soda
* 1/2 tsp salt
* 1/2 cup sugar
* 3/4 cup milk
* 1 egg, slightly beaten
* 1 Tbsp grated orange peel
* 1 Tbsp vegetable oil
* 1/2 cup whole wheat flour
* 1 cup coarsely chopped walnuts

Place the apricots on a chopping block. Sprinkle 1 T flour over them. Dip a knife into the flour and chop the apricots finely. Flour the knife often to keep the cut up fruit from sticking together. Sift the remaining flour, baking powder, baking soda, salt and sugar into a large bowl. Combine the milk, egg, orange peel, and oil. Stir the flour mixture and the whole wheat flour. Fold in the cut up apricots, any flour left on the cutting block and the walnuts. Pour into a well greased, floured baking unit. Cover and place on a rack in the slow cooker, but prop the lid open a fraction with a toothpick or a twist of foil to let excess steam escape.

Cook on High for 4 to 6 hours. Cool on a rack for 10 minutes. Serve warm or cold.

Makes 4 to 6 servings.

Now before you all ask what a baking unit is (I wondered as I sat and typed this in), I looked it up in the front of the bread section. She says that some manufacturers are making units for slow cookers, but if you don't have one, a 2 pound coffee can works. Pyrex muffin cups also work. Also 1, 1 1/2 and 2 quart molds work.

DO NOT LIFT THE LID WHILE BAKING THIS BREAD.

ARTICHOKE & CHEESE DIP
    * 1 lb. shredded Mozzarella
    * 1 c. grated Parmesan
    * 1 c. (8 oz. jar) mayonnaise
    * 1 c. (8 1/2 oz.) artichoke hearts, drained and chopped
    * Minced onions

Mix ingredients together. Bake in casserole at 350 degrees for 20-30 minutes or in lightly buttered 3 1/2 quart slow cooker/Crock Pot on (high) for about 1 hour.

Serve with broken up French bread or wheat crackers.

ASPARAGUS CASSEROLE
    2 cans sliced asparagus, (10 oz each)
    1 can cream of celery soup, (10 oz)
    2 hard cooked eggs, thinly sliced
    1 cup grated cheddar cheese
    1/2 cup coarsely crushed saltines or Ritz crackers
    1 teaspoon butter

Place drained asparagus in lightly buttered slow cooker/Crock Pot or slow cooker/Crock Pot baking insert. Combine soup and cheese. Top asparagus with sliced eggs, soup mixture, then the cracker crumbs. Dot with butter. Cover and cook on low for 4 to 6 hours.

BACON CHEESE DIP
* 16 slices bacon, diced, fried and drained
* 2 8-ounce packages cream cheese, softened and cubed
* 4 cups shredded cheddar cheese
* 1 cup half-and-half
* 2 teaspoons Worcestershire sauce
* 1 teaspoon dried minced onion
* 1/2 teaspoon dry mustard
* 1/2 teaspoon salt
* dash hot sauce

Put all ingredients in the Crock Pot and cook on low, stirring occasionally until cheese melts, about 1 hour. Taste and adjust seasonings, add bacon, and keep on low to serve.

Serve with cubed or sliced French bread.

BAKED APPLES (CROCKPOT)
* 6 lg. cooking apples
* 3/4 c. orange juice
* 2 tsp. grated orange rind
* 1 tsp. lemon rind grated
* 3/4 c. rose wine
* 1/4 tsp. cinnamon
* 1/2 c. brown sugar
* Whipped cream

Remove core from apples and place in slow cooker/Crock Pot. Mix together all other ingredients except whipped cream. Pour over apples. Cover pot and cook on low for about 3 1/2 hours or until apples are tender. Cool and serve with whipped cream.

BAKED CUSTARD
2 cups Milk, scalded
3 Eggs, slightly beaten
1/3 cup Sugar
1 teaspoon Vanilla
1/8 teaspoon Salt
Nutmeg or coconut

Scald milk, let cool slightly. Combine eggs, sugar, vanilla, and salt. Slowly stir in slightly cooled milk. Pour into buttered 1-qt baking dish. Sprinkle with nutmeg or coconut. Cover with foil.

Set baking dish on a trivet or meat rack in Crock Pot.

Pour hot water around baking dish, 1-inch deep. Cover pot and cook on high for 2 to 2 1/2 hours or until knife inserted in custard comes out clean. Serve warm or chilled.

Makes 5 to 6 servings.

BAKED HAM IN FOIL

Pour 1/2 cup water in Crock-Pot. Wrap precooked 3 to 4 pound ham in foil, place in Crock-Pot. Cover and cook on High 1 hour, then Low 6 to 7 hours or until ham is hot. If desired, sprinkle ham with liquid smoke before wrapping in foil.

If cooking larger ham, cook 1 hour on high then low 8 to 10 hours.

BAKED POTATOES

* 10 to 12 potatoes
* Aluminum foil

Prick potatoes with fork and wrap each in foil. Fill slow cooker/Crock Pot with potatoes. Cover and cook on low 8 to 10 hours. (High 2 1/4 to 4.) Do not add water.

BANANA BREAD

1 3/4 c flour
2 tsp baking powder
1/4 tsp baking soda
1/2 tsp salt
1/3 c shortening
2/3 c sugar
2 eggs, well beaten
1 1/2 c banana, well mashed, overripe
1/2 c walnuts, coarsely chopped

Sift together flour, baking powder, baking soda and salt. With electric beater on low, fluff shortening in a small bowl, until soft and creamy. Add sugar gradually. Beat in eggs in a slow stream. With a fork, beat in 1/3 of the flour mixture, ½ the bananas another 1/3 of the flour mixture, the rest of the bananas then the last of the flour mixture. Fold in walnuts. Turn into a greased and floured baking unit or a 2 1/2 quart mold and cover.

Place on a rack in crockpot. Cover crockpot, but prop the lid open with a toothpick or a twist of foil to let the excess steam escape. Cook on HIGH for 4 to 6 hours.

Cool on a rack for 10 minutes. Serve Warm.

BANANA NUT BREAD
1/3 c shortening
1/2 c sugar
2 eggs
1-3/4 c all purpose flour
1 tsp baking powder
1/2 tsp baking soda
1/2 tsp salt
1 c mashed ripe bananas
1/2 c chopped walnuts

Cream together shortening and sugar; add eggs and beat well. Sift dry ingreds; add to creamed mixture alternately with banana, blending well after each addition. Stir in nuts. Pour into well-greased 4-6 cup mold (I used a ceramic souffle dish). Cover with foil and tie a string tightly around it to keep foil down. Pour 2 cups hot water in slow-cooking pot. Place mold on rack or trivet (I modified a metal veggie steamer) in pot. Cover with crockpot lid and cook on high 2 to 3 hours or until bread is done. Be sure not to check bread during the first 2 hours of cooking.

BARBEQUE BEEF STEW
* 2 lbs. stew meat
* 3 tbsp. oil
* 1 c. onion, sliced
* 1/2 c. green pepper, chopped
* 1 lg. clove garlic
* 1/2 tsp. salt
* 1/8 tsp. pepper
* 2 c. beef stock
* 1 can (8 oz.) tomatoes
* 1 can (4 oz.) mushrooms
* 1/3 c. barbecue sauce

* 3 tbsp. cornstarch
* 1/4 c. cold water

Saute onion, pepper and garlic in oil. Add salt, pepper, beef stock, tomatoes, mushrooms and barbecue sauce. Cook in slow cooker/Crock Pot on low heat 8-10 hours.

Mix cornstarch, cold water and thicken before serving. Serve over hot cooked rice.

BARBECUE BRISKET
First, make a batch of homemade Bar-Be-Que Sauce:
1 TBS liquid smoke
1 TBS crushed garlic (or less, we like lots)
1 large onion chopped (I use a small vidalia)
2 TBS cider venegar
1 TBS loose brown sugar (not packed)
3 TBS fresh squeezed lemon juice
1-14 oz. bottle of ketchup
1/2 tsp chili powder
4 TBS worchestershire
1 TBS dry mustard powder (like Coleman's)
1 cup water or red wine
1 tsp salt
1/8 tsp black pepper
1 TBS honey
Mix together and heat on range.

Then prep the brisket by removing all silver skin if the butchere didn't already do this, place it in the CP, pour the homemade sauce over it and let it go on low. The length of time cooking will depend on how large a brisket you got. When done, remove lid from CP and using two forks shred the brisket. Terrific served on rolls or buns. It's also good served like tacos with all the trimmings in soft or regular taco shells.

BARBECUE CHICKEN I
1 Chicken, cut up and skin removed
1 cup ketchup
3/4 cup brown sugar
3 tablespoons Worcestershire sauce

Place chicken in crockpot. Combine remaining ingredients and pour over chicken.

Cook 4 hours on high or 8-10 hours on low. Delicious!

BARBECUE CHICKEN II
4-6 pieces chicken (I use boneless breasts)
1 bottle BBQ sauce
1/2 cup white vinegar
1/2 cup brown sugar
1 tsp. mesquite seasoning
1/2 tsp. garlic powder
1/2-1 tsp. red pepper flakes

Mix BBQ sauce with all ingredients listed under it. Place chicken in crockpot. Pour sauce over all. Cook slowly in crockpot about 4-6 hours. Serve with baked beans, potato salad and coleslaw.

NOTE: Since this didn't specify whether it should be on high or low, the first time I cooked on high for 5 hours. The chicken was dry as dirt :(The 2nd time, I cooked it on low for 4 1/2 hours and it was perfect.

BARBECUE CHICKEN III
1 frying chicken cut up or quartered
1 can condensed tomato soup
3/4 cup chopped onion
1/4 cup vinegar
3 Tablespoons brown sugar
1 Tablespoon Worcestershire sauce
1/2 teaspoon salt
1/4 teaspoon sweet basil
1/4 teaspoon thyme

Place chicken in slow cooker. Combine all other ingredients and pour over chicken.

Cover tightly and cook at "low" for 6-8 hours. Makes 4 servings.

BARBECUE PORK ROAST
1 pork roast (or beef)
Juice of 1 lemon
1 small onion, cut up

1 teaspoon sugar
1 bottle barbecue sauce
Cook roast covered in water (start with hot water) in crockpot overnight on low 10-12 hours. Pour off water and pull meat into shredded pieces. Saute onion in a little butter. Combine barbecue sauce, onions, sugar and juice of lemon with meat in crockpot and cook on high for 1 1/2 to 2 1/2 hours, or on low for 3 to 6 hours.

BARBECUE PORK SANDWICHES
1 pork roast
1 bottle bar-b-cue sauce
About 1/2 to 1 cup water
Just throw in crockpot on high for about 6 hrs. or low for about 10 hrs.
When it's done, just remove meat from bone and serve on hamburger buns or rolls with more bar-b-que sauce or ketchup, etc.

BARBECUE SAUCE
1 cup chopped celery
1 medium onion chopped
1 Tbsp. butter
Saute until golden brown.
2 Tbsp. vinegar
1 Tbsp. brown sugar
3 Tbsp. Worcestershire sauce
1 Tbsp. lemon juice
1 tsp. salt (optional)
1 tsp. mustard
1 cup ketchup
1 cup water
2 lbs. ground beef
Combine all ingredients in a large saucepan. Cook slowly for 2 -21/2 hours. (Is better reheated)

BARBECUE STEAK
1 1/2 lb boneless chuck steak, 1 1/2" thick
1 clove garlic, peeled and minced
1/4 cup wine vinegar
1 Tbsp brown sugar

1 tsp paprika
2 Tbsp Worcestershire sauce
1/2 cup catsup (ketchup)
1 tsp salt
1 tsp dry or prepared mustard
1/4 tsp black pepper

Cut the beef on a diagonal, across the grain into slices 1" wide. Place these in the crockpot. In a small bowl, combine the remaining ingredients. Pour over the meat, and mix. Cover and cook on Low for 3 to 5 hours.

BARBECUED BEAN SOUP

* 1 lb Great Northern beans, soaked
* 2 tsp Salt
* 1 med Onion, chopped
* 1/8 tsp Ground pepper
* 2 lb Beef short ribs
* 6 cup Water
* 3/4 cup Barbecue sauce

Place all ingredients in Slow Cooker except barbecue sauce Cover and cook on Low 10 to 16 hours. Before serving, remove short ribs and cut meat from bones. Return meat to Slow Cooker. Stir in barbecue sauce before serving.

BARBECUED COCKTAIL MEATBALLS

* 2 lbs. lean ground beef
* 1 1/3 C ketchup, divided
* 3 T seasoned dry bread crumbs
* 1 egg, slightly beaten
* 2 T dried onion flakes
* 3/4 t garlic salt
* 1/2 t black pepper
* 1 C packed brown sugar
* 1 can (6 oz) tomato paste
* 1/4 C reduced-sodium soy sauce
* 1/4 C cider vinegar
* 1 1/2 t hot pepper sauce

Preheat oven to 350 degrees. Combine ground beef, 1/3 cup ketchup, bread crumbs, egg onion flakes, garlic sale, and black pepper in medium bowl. Mix lightly but thoroughly; shape into 1-inch meatballs. Place meatballs in two 15 x 10" jelly-roll pans or shallow roasting pans. Bake 18 minutes or until browned. Transfer meatballs to slow cooker. (YOU CAN SKIP THIS WHOLE PARAGRAPH IF YOU BUY THE FROZEN MEATBALLS FROM SAM'S WHOLESALE CLUB – THEY'RE WONDERFUL! :)

Mix remaining 1 cup ketchup, sugar, tomato paste, soy sauce, vinegar, and hot pepper sauce in medium bowl. Pour over meatballs. Cover and cook on LOW 4 hours.

Serve with cocktail picks.

Makes about 4 dozen meatballs.

BARBECUED MEATBALLS I
* 1 to 2 lbs. ground beef
* 2 tsp. Worcestershire sauce
* 2/3 c. evaporated milk
* 1 envelope dry onion soup mix
Sauce:
* 2 c. ketchup
* 1 c. brown sugar, packed
* 1 tbsp. Worcestershire sauce

Mix beef, 2 teaspoons Worcestershire sauce, evaporated milk and soup mix. Shape into balls the size of walnuts. Broil 4 inches from broiler for 12 minutes or until done. Turn if necessary to keep from burning. Mix sauce ingredients and boil 10 minutes. Pour over meat-balls in slow cooker/Crock Pot turned on low.

2 pounds of ground beef makes about 50 meatballs.

BARBECUED MEATBALLS II
* 2 pounds ground beef
* 1 cup bread crumbs
* 1 teaspoon garlic powder
* 2 packages onion soup mix
* 2 teaspoons Worcestershire sauce
* 2 eggs
Sauce:
* 2 onions, chopped
* 2 cans tomato paste (12 ounces total)

* 2 cloves garlic, minced
* 1/4 cup Worcestershire sauce
* 1/4 cup red wine vinegar
* 1/2 cup brown sugar
* 1/2 cup sweet pickle relish
* 1/2 cup beef broth
* 2 teaspoons salt
* 2 teaspoons dry mustard

Combine first 6 ingredients and mix well. Shape into meatballs and brown in a skillet with 1 tablespoon of oil. Drain on paper towels.

Add all sauce ingredients to Crock Pot and stir well. Add meatballs and cook, covered, on low for 5 to 6 hours (high for 2 to 3). Serve from the Crock Pot.

Makes about 60 meatballs.

BARBECUED PORK STRIPS

* 1/2 cup soy sauce
* 1/4 cup dry sherry
* 1/2 cup brown sugar
* 2 cloves garlic, crushed
* 1/8 teaspoon pepper
* 1/2 cup barbecue sauce
* 1 8-ounce can pineapple chunks (do not drain)
* 3 pounds lean pork, cut into strips, browned, and drained

Combine all ingredients except pork strips in Crock Pot and stir well. Add pork and stir to coat. Cook on low, covered, for 8 to 10 hours. Serve with sauce.

Makes about 15 servings.

BARLEY WITH MUSHROOMS & GREEN ONIONS

1 cup barley
1 can (14 1/2 oz) roasted garlic chicken broth (about 2 cups)
3 green onions, thinly sliced (about 1/2 cup)
4 to 6 ounces fresh or canned mushrooms, sliced
salt or seasoned salt and pepper to taste
2 teaspoons butter or margarine

Combine all ingredients in slow cooker/Crock Pot. Cover and cook on low for 4 to 4 1/2 hours.

BAVARIAN RED CABBAGE
* 1 large head of red cabbage, washed and coarsely sliced
* 2 medium onions coarsely chopped
* 6 tart apples, cored & quartered
* 2 tsp. salt
* 2 cups hot water
* 3 TBSP sugar
* 2/3 cup cider vinegar
* 6 TBSP bacon grease or butter

Place all ingredients in the Crock-Pot in order listed. Cover and cook on low 8 to 10 hours (High: 3 hours). Stir well before serving.

BAYOU GUMBO
* 3 tablespoons Pillsbury Best All Purpose Flour
* 3 tablespoons oil
* 1/2 pound smoked sausage, cut into 1/2 inch slices
* 2 cups frozen cut okra
* 1 large onion, chopped
* 1 large green bell pepper, chopped
* 3 garlic cloves, minced
* 1/4 teaspoon ground red pepper (cayenne)
* 1/4 teaspoon pepper
* 1 (14.5 ounce) can diced tomatoes, undrained
* 1 (12-ounce) package frozen shelled deveined cooked medium shrimp, rinsed
* 1 1/2 cups uncooked regular long-grain white rice
* 3 cups water

In small saucepan, combine flour and oil; mix well. Cook, stirring constantly, over
medium-high heat for 5 minutes. Reduce heat to medium; cook, stirring constantly, about 10 minutes or until mixture turns reddish brown. Place flour-oil mixture in 3 1/2 to 4 quart Slow Cooker. Stir in all remaining ingredients except shrimp, rice and water. Cover; cook on low setting for 7-9 hours. When ready to serve, cook rice in water as directed on package. Meanwhile, add shrimp to gumbo mixture in slow cooker/Crock Pot; mix well. Cover; cook on low setting for additional 20 minutes.

Serve gumbo over rice.

Makes 6 servings.

BEER MEATBALLS
* 1 can of beer
* 1 6 oz can spicy V-8 juice
* 1 tsp. lemon juice
* 1 tsp. hot sauce
* 1/2 c. Italian bread crumbs
* 1 c. onions
* Salt and pepper to taste
* 1 lg. bottle ketchup
* 1 tsp. horseradish
* 1 tsp. Worcestershire sauce
* 2 to 3 lbs. ground beef
* 2 to 3 eggs

Combine ground beef, 1/2 cup onions, Italian bread crumbs, eggs. Make the mixture into small meatballs. Then fry or bake the meat. In saucepan combine remaining ingredients. Simmer for 15 minutes. Put meatballs and sauce into slow cooker/Crock Pot. The sauce should cover the meat. Allow to simmer in slow cooker/Crock Pot for at least 3 hours, however, the longer you let them simmer, the better they are! 6 to 10 hours on low temperature is great. Stir them occasionally. You may wish to add more ketchup, or V-8 juice - spice them up if you like them hot.

BEST DIP EVER
* 1 (1 pound) package Velveeta
* 1 can Chili - no beans
* 1 pound medium or spicy sausage, browned and crumbled

You can heat this on the stove until the cheese melts and it all mixes together OR I usually put it in the Crock Pot on low until blended and then keep it there to serve.

BLACK BEAN CHILI
1 # dry black beans
2 T. oil
6 garlic cloves, minced or pressed
2 onions, chopped
1/4 t. crushed red pepper flakes (more if you like hot food)

1 T. chili powder
1 T. ground cumin
1 t. dried oregano
1 bay leaf
1 28 oz. can chopped tomatoes in juice
1 T. soy sauce
2 c. water
6 oz. can tomato paste
1 T. red wine vinegar
2 cans contrasting beans (pinto, garbanzo, great northern, etc.)--drained and rinsed garnishes: grated cheese, sour cream, chopped parsley, onion, etc.

Rinse and sort the beans and place in the slow cooker/Crock Pot with a generous amount of water.

Cook on low overnight (no presoaking necessary). In the morning drain the cooking water. Heat the oil in a skillet and saute the onions, garlic and red pepper flakes. Cook 1 minute, then add chili powder and cumin and cook 2 minutes, stirring.

Add this mixture to the slow cooker/Crock Pot along with all remaining ingredients except canned beans and garnishes. Stir well and cook on low all day. Stir in canned beans an hour or so before serving. Serve with garnishes.

BLACK BEAN SOUP
* 2 onion, chopped
* 2 cloves garlic, minced
* 3 tablespoons butter
* 1 pound black beans, soaked overnight,
* drained
* 1 ham bone, cracked
* 1 stalk celery, chopped
* 1 bay leaf
* 1/2 cup sherry, or dry white wine
* salt and pepper, to taste

Saute onions and garlic in butter until transparent. combine with beans, hame bone, celery, bay leaf, and 2 quarts water in the Crock Pot. Cook on high, covered for 2 hours, then on low for 8 to 10 hours. Remove ham bone and bay leaf. Puree soup and return to pot.

Add sherry, salt and pepper and heat through. Serve in soup bowls garnished with chopped hard-boiled eggs, parsley, and lemon slices.

BOILED PEANUTS
1 1/2 quarts green uncooked peanuts
1/2 cup salt
2 1/2 quarts water
Wash Peanuts until water runs clear. Put clean peanuts in crockery pot, add salt and water; stir.

Cook, covered, on high for 5 to 7 hours. Add additional water during cooking, if necessary, to keep peanuts covered.

BREAKFAST COBBLER
* 4 medium-sized apples -- peeled and sliced
* 1/4 cup honey
* 1 tsp cinnamon
* 2 tablespoons butter -- melted
* 2 cups granola cereal
Place apples in slow cooker and mix in remaining ingredients. Cover and cook on low 7-9 hours (overnight) or on high 2-3 hours. Serve with milk.

Yield: 4 servings

Broccoli & Cheese Soup
2 c. cooked noodles
1 (10 oz.) pkg. frozen chopped broccoli,thawed
3 tbsp. chopped onions
2 tbsp. butter
1 tbsp. flour
2 cups shredded American cheese
Salt to taste
5 1/2 c. milk
Combine all ingredients in slow cooker. Stir well. Cook on low for 4 hours.

8 servings.

BROCCOLI CHEESE DIP
* 2 (10 oz.) boxes of frozen chopped broccoli
* 2 cans cream of mushroom soup

* 1/4 c. sour cream
* 1/2 lb. Mexican Velveeta cheese
* 1/2 lb. reg. Velveeta cheese
* 1 tbsp. garlic salt

Cook and drain broccoli. Melt cheese in slow cooker/Crock Pot. Mix soups, sour cream, broccoli and garlic salt. Mix into melted cheese. Serve as dip with tortilla chips.

BROCCOLI DIP
* 1 pkg.(10oz) frozen chopped broccoli
* 2 ribs celery, chopped
* 1 med. white onion, chopped
* 3/4 stick margarine
* 2 rolls garlic cheese
* 1 can cream of mushroom soup
* 1 med. can mushroom pieces
* 1 can sliced water chestnuts
* 2 tsp. Worcestershire sauce

Cook broccoli until tender. Saute celery and onion in oleo until tender. Place broccoli and sauteed vegetables in slow cooker/Crock Pot; add mushrooms, cheese, cream of mushroom soup. Stir well and heat on low until cheese is melted. Add water chestnuts and Worcestershire sauce. Serve warm in the slow cooker/Crock Pot, with chips or crackers.

BROCCOLI SOUFFLE
2 pkgs. frozen chopped broccoli (2 lbs.)
1 can cream of celery soup (undiluted)
1 c. real mayonnaise
3 tbsp. grated onion
2 eggs, beaten
1 c. grated cheddar cheese
Ritz crackers
1 stick melted margarine

Cook broccoli; drain and cool. Mix soup, mayonnaise, onion, egg, and cheese and add to cooled broccoli. Put in a lightly greased 3 1/2-quart crockery cooker. Mix 1 stack Ritz or buttery crackers (crushed) with margarine or butter. Put on top. Cook on high for 2 to

3 hours.

BRUNSWICK STEW
1 Chicken, 3 lbs, cut up
2 quarts Water
1 Onion, chopped
2 cups Ham; cooked, cubed
3 Potatoes, diced
2 cans Tomatoes; 16 oz, ea, cut up
10 ounces Lima beans, frozen and thawed
10 ounces Corn; whole kernel, frozen, partially thawed
2 teaspoons Salt
1 teaspoon Sugar
1/4 teaspoon Pepper
1/2 teaspoon Seasoned salt

In a slow cooker/Crock Pot combine chicken with water, onion, ham, amd potatoes. Cook covered on LOW for 4 to 5 hours or until chicken is done. Lift chicken out of pot; remove meat from bones. Return chicken meat to pot.

Add tomatoes, beans, corn, salt, seasoned salt, sugar and pepper. Cover and Cook on HIGH 1 hour.

Makes 8 servings.

CAJUN BREW PORK N BEANS
5 cans Pork-n-Beans (2nd to smallest size)
2 8oz cans tomatoe sauce
2 onions (chopped)
6 hot links (sliced)
1/4 bottle barbeque sauce (average size)
The following are "to taste"
Worcestershire sauce
Hot sauce (I like Crystal hot sauce)
Cajun Seasonings (I like Tony Chacere's seasonings)
Liquid smoke
Mustard
Brown Sugar

Mix all ingredients in a crockpot and crank it up to high. Let it cook all day, stirring occasionally.

Can also be made on the stove top, but let it simmer for several hours stirring occasionally.

CAJUN PECANS
1 pound pecan halves
4 Tbs butter, melted
1 Tbs chili powder
1 tsp salt
1 tsp dried basil
1 tsp dried oregano
1 tsp dried thyme
1/2 tsp onion powder
1/4 tsp garlic powder
1/4 tsp cayenne pepper
Combine all ingredients in Crock Pot. Cover and cook on high for 15 minutes. Turn on low, uncovered, stirring occasionally for 2 hours. Transfer nuts to a baking sheet and cool completely.

CAMP STEW
* 1 can bar-b-que beef
* 1 can bar-b-que chicken
* 1 can bar-b-que pork
* 1 can stewed tomatoes
* 1 can corn
* 3 c. cubed potatoes
* 1 onion, chopped
Cube potatoes, chopped onion. Cook until partly tender. Place in slow cooker/Crock Pot. Open all cans and add to slow cooker/Crock Pot, stir. Cook for at least an hour. Serve with corn sticks or bread sticks.

CANDIED BANANAS
* 6 green-tipped bananas, peeled
* 1/2 cup flaked coconut
* 1/2 tsp cinnamon
* 1/4 tsp salt
* 1/2 cup dark corn syrup
* 1/4 cup butter or margarine, melted

* 2 tsp grated lemon peel
* 1/4 cup lemon juice

1.. Put bananas and coconut into large enough CP to fit in single layer. Sprinkle with cinnamon and salt.

2.. Mix corn syrup, butter ,lemon peel, and lemon juice; pour over bananas.

3.. Cover and cook on Low 1 to 2 hours.

CANNELLINI ALLA CATANIA

1 lb Dried canellini beans (white kidney beans)
use white northern if unable to find canellini
6 c Water
2 Hot Italian sausages, sliced
1 lg Onion, chopped
1 lg Garlic clove, minced
2 lg Tomatoes, ripe, peeled and coarsley chopped
1 Bay leaf, crumbled
1/2 ts Thyme, crumbled
1/2 ts Basil, crumbled
3 Strips of orange rind (1in)
1 ts Salt
1/4 ts Pepper
1 ts Instant beef broth

-Pick over beans and rinse. Cover beans with water in a large kettle; bring to boiling; cover; cook 2 minutes; remove from heat; let stand 1 hour. Pour into an electric slow cooker.

-Brown sausages in a small skillet; push to one side; saute onion and garlic in same pan until soft; stir in tomato, bay leaf, thyme, basil, orange strips, salt and pepper and instant beef broth; bring to boiling; stir into beans; cover.

-Cook on low for 10 hours or on high for 5 hours or until beans are tender. YIELD:
6 servings

CARAMEL NUT ROLLS

2 8 oz. pkgs. refrigerator biscuits
1/4 c. melted butter or margarine

1/2 c. brown sugar
1/4 c. chopped nuts
Cinnamon

Mix brown sugar and nuts together. Dip each refrigerator biscuit in melted butter, then brown sugar and nuts.

Place in Rival Bread and Cake pan or a 3 pound coffee can. Sprinkle each layer of biscuits with cinnamon. If using coffee can, cover with several layers of paper towels. Cook on high for 3-4 hours. No peeking! You can check bread after two hours.

You can use yeast rolls--frozen, unbaked--which may be thawed and substituted for the refrigerator biscuits. Fill your can and pan with 16 oz. of dipped rolls and let rise for 30 minutes before baking. Bake as directed for 3-4 hours.

CARAMEL RUM FONDUE

7 ounces Caramels
1/4 cup Miniature marshmallows
1/3 cup Whipping cream
2 teaspoons Rum or 1/4 tsp rum extract

Combine caramels and cream in Crock Pot. Cover and heat until melted, 30 to 60 minutes. Stir in marshmallows and rum. Cover and continue cooking 30 minutes.

Serve with apple wedges or pound cake.

CARMEL APPLES

* 2 packages (14oz) bags caramels
* 1/4 cup Water
* 8 Medium apples

In slow cooker/Crock Pot, combine caramels and water. Cover and cook on high for 1 to 1 1/2 hours, stirring frequently. Wash and dry apples. Insert stick into stem end of each apple. Turn control on low. Dip apple into hot caramel and turn to coat entire surface. Holding apple above pot, scrape off excess accumulation of caramel from bottom apple.

Place on greased wax paper to cool.

CARROT PUDDING
* 4 large carrots, cooked and grated
* 1 small onion, grated
* 1/2 teaspoon salt
* 1/4 teaspoon nutmeg
* 1 tablespoon sugar
* 1 cup milk
* 3 eggs, beaten

Mix together carrots, onion, salt, nutmeg, sugar, milk, and eggs. Pour into slow cooker and cook on high for 3-4 hours.

CASSEROLE IN THE COOKER
1 package (16 oz) frozen broccoli cuts, thawed and drained
3 cp cubed fully cooked ham
1 can condensed cream of mushroom soup, undiluted
1 jar (8 oz) process cheese sauce
1 cp milk
1 cp uncooked instant rice
1 celery rib, chopped
1 small onion, chopped

In a slow cooker, combine broccoli and ham. Combine the soup, cheese sauce, milk, rice, celery and onion; stir into the broccoli mixture. Cover and cook on low 4-5 hours or until rice is tender.

4 servings.

CHEDDAR POTATO SLICES
1 can (10 3/4 ounces) Campbell's® Condensed Cream of Mushroom Soup
1/2 teaspoon paprika
1/2 teaspoon pepper
4 medium baking potatoes (about 1 1/4 pounds), sliced 1/4-inch thick
1 cup shredded cheddar cheese (4 ounces)

1. Mix soup, paprika and pepper. In greased 2-quart shallow baking dish arrange potatoes in overlapping rows. Sprinkle with cheese. Spoon soup mixture over cheese.

2. Cover and bake at 400°F. for 45 minutes. Uncover and bake 10 minutes more or until potatoes
are tender. Serves 6.
For the slow cooker/Crock Pot:
Follow directions above, placing ingredients in a lightly greased slow cooker/Crock Pot. Cover and cook on high for 3 to 4 hours, until potatoes are tender. Keep warm (on low) for serving.

CHEESE AND POTATO CASSEROLE
2 lb. pkg. frozen hash brown potatoes (partially thawed)
2 (10 oz.) cans cheddar cheese soup
1 (13 oz.) can evaporated milk
1 can French fried onion rings, divided
Salt and pepper to taste
Combine potatoes, soup, milk, and half the can of onion rings; pour into greased slow cooker/Crock Pot and add salt and pepper. Cover and cook on low for 8 to 9 hours or high for 4 hours. Sprinkle the rest of the onion rings of top before serving.

CHEESE & ARTICHOKE DIP
* 8 ounces process American cheese (Velveeta)
* 1 can (10oz) 98% fat-free cream of mushroom soup
* 2 teaspoons Worcestershire sauce
* 1/4 cup evaporated milk
* 1 teaspoon dry mustard
* 1 1/2 cups shredded cheddar cheese
* 1/3 cup chopped roasted red pepper
* 1 can artichoke hearts, drained and coarsely chopped
Combine all ingredients in the slow cooker/Crock Pot. Cover and cook on low for 2 to 3 hours, until melted. Stir well and serve with assorted crackers, bread cubes, or chips.
You can also use this dip with cooked pasta for a delicious macaroni and cheese!

CHEESY CAULIFLOWER AND BROCCOLI
1 (10 oz) pkg frozen cauliflower, thawed
1 (10 oz) pkg frozen broccoli, thawed
1 can Cheddar cheese soup
4 slices bacon

salt and pepper to taste

1/4 cup shredded cheddar cheese, if desired

Fry bacon until crisp; drain well on paper towels then crumble. Place broccoli and cauliflower in crockery pot. Top with soup, sprinkle with bacon. Season with salt and pepper. Cover and cook on low for 4 to 5 hours. About 20 minutes before done, top with cheddar cheese if used.

Serves 6 to 8.

CHEESY CROCKPOT CHICKEN I

3 whole boneless chicken breasts

2 cans cream chicken soup

1 can chedder cheese soup

Remove all fat and skin from chicken; rinse and pat dry, sprinkle with salt, pepper and garlic powder. Put in crockpot and add the three soups straight from the cans.

Cook on low all day (at least 8 hrs) do not lift the lid. Serve over rice or noodles. We did noodles and hubby said it tasted like mac and cheese.

CHEESY CROCKPOT CHICKEN II

6 chicken breasts (boneless & skinless)

salt & pepper to taste

garlic powder, to taste

2 cans cream of chicken soup

1 can cheddar cheese soup

Rinse chicken and sprinkle with salt, pepper and garlic powder. Mix undiluted soup and pour over chicken in the crock pot. Cook on low 6 to 8 hours. Serve over rice or noodles.

Serving Suggestion: Serve over rice.

CHEESY CROCKPOT CHICKEN AND VEGETABLES

1/3 c. diced canadian bacon or ham

2-3 carrots, sliced or chopped

2-3 celery ribs, sliced or chopped

1 small onion, sliced or chopped

2 cans mushrooms or 1/4 lb fresh, sliced

1 can green beans, drained very well

1/4 c. water

Layer in crock pot in order given.

2-3 lbs. chicken, cut up. Put on top of veggies, largest pieces first.

2 tsp. chicken bouillon granules

1 Tbs. chopped fresh parsley

3/4 tsp. poultry seasoning

-Mix together and sprinkle over chicken pieces.

1 can condensed cheddar cheese soup

1 Tbs. flour

1/4 c. parmesan cheese

-Mix together and drop on top of chicken, DO NOT STIR.

Cover and cook on high 3-4 hours, or low 6-8 hours.

-Make noodles OR rice OR mashed potatoes to serve over.

This is a very versatile dish, use more/less/different veggies (I often clean out the fridge into the crockpot for this) and if the sauce is too thin you can thicken with a little cornstarch or parmesan cheese before serving.

CHERRY COBBLER

1 16 oz can cherry pie filling, light

1 pkg cake mix for 1 layer cake, or sweet muffin mix

1 egg

3 tablespoons evaporated milk

1/2 teaspoon cinnamon

1/2 cup chopped nuts, optional

Put pie filling in lightly buttered 3 1/2-quart Crock Pot and cook on high for 30 minutes. Mix together the remaining ingredients and spoon onto the hot pie filling. Cover and cook for 2 to 3 hours on low. You may also use a lightly greased souffle dish in a larger Crock Pot.

6 servings.

CHERRY CRISP

1 can (21 oz) cherry pie filling

2/3 cup brown sugar

1/2 cup quick-cooking oats

1/2 cup flour

1 teaspoon brown sugar

1/3 cup butter, softened

Lightly butter a 3 1/2-quart slow cooker/Crock Pot. Place cherry pie filling in the slow cooker/Crock Pot. Combine dry ingredients and mix well; cut in butter with a pastry cutter or fork. Sprinkle crumbs over the cherry pie filling. Cook for 5 hours on low.

CHICKEN A LA KING
* 1 1/2 to 2 pounds boneless chicken tenders
* 1 to 1 1/2 cup matchstick-cut carrots
* 1 bunch green onions (scallions) sliced in 1/2-inch pieces
* 1 jar Kraft pimiento or pimiento & olive process cheese spread (5oz)
* 1 can 98% fat-free cream of chicken soup
* 2 tablespoons dry sherry (optional)
* salt and pepper to taste

Put all ingredients in the slow cooker/Crock Pot (3 1/2-quart or larger) in the order given; stir to combine. Cover and cook on low for 7 to 9 hours. Serve over rice, toast, or biscuits.

Serves 6 to 8.

CHICKEN CACCIATORE IN CROCKPOT
Place cut up chicken in slow cooker/Crock Pot, cover with one large undrained can of cut-up tomatoes, one cut-up onion, one cut-up green pepper, minced garlic (to taste), one Tbs. Italian herbs, red pepper flakes to taste. (I add mushrooms if I have them!) Cook all on low 6-8 hours until falling apart. Serve over hubby's favorite pasta, sprinkling more pepper flakes (if you dare!) and plenty of Parmesan cheese over it!

CHICKEN CASSEROLE
1 8oz pkg noodles
3 cups diced cooked chicken
1/2 cup diced celery
1/2 cup diced green pepper
1/2 cup diced onion
1 4 oz can mushrooms
1 4 oz jar pimiento

1/2 cup parmesan cheese
1 1/2 cups cream style cottage cheese
1 cup grated charp process cheese
1 can cream of chicken soup
1/2 cup chicken broth
2 Tbsp. melted butter
1/2 tsp. basil

Cook noodles according to pkg directions and drain and rinse thoroughly. In a large bowl, combine remaining ingredients with noodles until well mixed. Pour mixture into greased crockpot. COver and cook on low for 6-8 hours or high 3-4 hours.

Serves 6

Chicken Chili

2 whole chicken breasts, skinned,
deboned, cut in 1/2" chunks
Celery heart
1 med. onion
2 cans stewed tomatoes, sliced
16 oz. med. salsa or picante sauce
1 can chick peas (or 1 pkg. pkg.
white kidney beans)
6 oz. mushrooms
Olive oil

Brown chicken in 1 tablespoon olive oil. Chop celery, onion and mushrooms. Combine all ingredients in large slow cooker/Crock Pot, stir and simmer on low heat for 6-8 hours. Serve with bread or taco chips. *If you like it spicy, use hot salsa or picante sauce.

CHICKEN MERLOT WITH MUSHROOMS

2 1/2 to 3 lbs. meaty chicken pieces, skinned
3 c. sliced fresh mushrooms
1 large onion, chopped
2 cloves garlic, minced
3/4 c. chicken broth
1 6-ounce can tomato paste
1/4 c. dry red wine (such as Merlot) or chicken broth (I used broth)
2 tbsp. quick-cooking tapioca

2 tbsp. snipped fresh basil or 1 1/2 tsp. dried basil, crushed (I used dried)

2 tsp. sugar

1/4 tsp. salt

1/4 tsp. pepper

2 c. hot cooked noodles

2 tbsp. finely shredded Parmesan cheese (I used the kind in a shaker)

Rinse chicken; set aside. In a 3 1/2-4-or 5-quart crockery cooker place mushrooms, onion, and garlic. Place chicken pieces on top of the vegetables. In a bowl combine broth, tomato paste, wine or chicken broth, tapioca, dried basil (if using), sugar, salt, and pepper. Pour over all. Cover; cook on low-heat setting for 7 to 8 hours or on high-heat setting for 3 ½ to 4 hours. If using, stir in fresh basil. To serve, spoon chicken, mushroom mixture, and sauce over hot cooked noodles Sprinkle with Parmesan cheese.

Makes 4 to 6 servings.

Prep time: 25 min.

CHICKEN OR TURKEY PIE

3 cups diced cooked chicken or turkey

2 cans (14 1/2 ounce each) chicken broth

1/2 teaspoon salt

1/2 teaspoon pepper

1 stalk celery, thinly sliced

1 medium onion, chopped

1 bay leaf

3 cups potatoes, peeled and cubed

1 package frozen mixed veggies (16 oz)

1 cup milk

1 cup flour

1 teaspoon pepper

1/2 teaspoon salt

1 9-inch refrigerated pie crust

In Crock Pot, combine chicken, broth, 1/2 teaspoon salt, 1/2 teaspoon pepper, celery, onion, bay leaf, potatoes, and mixed vegetables. Cover and cook on low 8 to 10 hours or on high 4 to 6 hours. Remove bay leaf. Pre heat oven to 400 degrees. In a small bowl, mix milk and flour. Gradually stir flour and water mixture into Crock Pot. Stir in pepper, poultry seasoning, and salt/ Remove the liner from Crock

Pot base and carefully place 9-inch pie crust over the mixture. Place the crockery liner inside preheated oven and bake (uncovered) for about 15 minutes, or until browned. If your liner is not removable, put the mixture in a casserole dish, cover with the pie crust and bake as above.

Serves 8.

CHICKEN SOUP
2 Onions, chopped
3 Carrots, sliced
2 Stalks celery, sliced
2 teaspoons Salt
1/4 teaspoon Pepper
1/2 teaspoon Basil
1/4 teaspoon Leaf thyme
3 tablespoons Dry parsley flakes
1 package Frozen peas (10 oz.)
1 2-1/2 to 3 lb. whole fryer
4 cups Water or chicken stock
1 cup Noodles

Place all ingredients in slow cooker/Crock Pot, except noodles, in order listed. Cover and cook on LOW 8 to 10 hours, or HIGH 4 to 6 hours. One hour before serving, remove chicken and cool slightly. Remove meat from bones and return meat to slow cooker/Crock Pot. Add noodles. Turn to HIGH. Cover and cook 1 hour.

CHICKEN WINGS IN BBQ SAUCE
* 3 pounds chicken wings (16 wings)
* salt and pepper to taste
* 1 1/2 cups any variety barbecue sauce
* 1/4 cup honey
* 2 teaspoons prepared mustard or spicy mustard
* 2 teaspoons Worcestershire sauce
* Tabasco to taste, optional

Rinse chicken and pat dry. Cut off and discard wing tips. Cut each wing at joint to make two sections. Sprinkle wing parts with salt and pepper. Place wings on a broiler pan. Broil 4-5 inches from the heat for 20 minutes, 10 minutes for each side or until chicken is brown. Transfer chicken to slow cooker/Crock Pot. For sauce, combine barbecue sauce, honey, mustard, Worcestershire sauce and if more

heat is desired...Tabasco to taste in a small mixing bowl. Pour over chicken wings. Cover and cook on low for 4-5 hours or on High 2 -2 1/2 hours. Serve directly from slow cooker/Crock Pot. Makes about 32 appetizers.

CHICKEN WINGS IN TERIYAKI SAUCE
   * 3 pounds chicken wings (16 wings)
   * 1 large onion, chopped
   * 1 cup soy sauce
   * 1 cup brown sugar
   * 2 teaspoons ground ginger
   * 2 cloves garlic, minced
   * 1/4 cup dry cooking sherry

Rinse chicken and pat dry. Cut off and discard wing tips. Cut each wing at joint to make two sections. Place wing parts on broiler pan. Broil 4-5 inches from the heat for 20 minutes, 10 minutes for each side or until chicken is brown. Transfer chicken to slow cooker/Crock Pot. Mix together onion, soy sauce, brown sugar, ginger, garlic and cooking sherry in bowl. Pour over chicken wings. Cover and cook on Low 5-6 hours or on HIGH 2-3 hours. Stir chicken wings once to ensure wings are evenly coated with sauce. Serve from Slow Cooker. Makes about 32 pieces

CHILI
   2 lbs. ground beef
   1 lg. onion
   1 lg. green pepper
   1 lg. jalapeno pepper
   Chili powder to taste
   Garlic salt to taste
   Salt to taste
   Pepper to taste

Sugar to taste
2 cans crushed tomatoes
1 can tomato puree
1 can kidney beans
2 cans chili hot beans
Brown beef. Saute chopped onion and green pepper in grease. Mix beef, onion and green pepper. Add spices; let stand 1 hour. Add tomatoes, tomato puree, beans; cook in Crock Pot all day. Best if refrigerated and warmed the next day.

CHILI BEEF DIP

* 1 (11 oz.) can condensed chili beef soup
* 3 oz. pkg. cream cheese, softened
* 1/2 cup sour cream
* 1 tbsp. water
* 1 teaspoon prepared mustard
* 1 teaspoon Worcestershire sauce
* 1/2 teaspoon chili sauce
* 1/4 teaspoon hot pepper sauce, optional

In slow cooker/Crock Pot, combine all ingredients; mix well. Cover and cook on low for 1 1/2 to 2 hours, stirring occasionally, or until cheese is melted and dip is hot. Serve warm with tortilla or corn chips.
Makes 2 cups.

CHILI CHEESE TACO DIP

* 1 lb. hamburger
* 1 can chili (no beans)
* 1 lb. mild Mexican Velveeta cheese, cubed or shredded

Brown hamburger; drain and place in slow cooker. Add chili and cheese; cover and cook on low until cheese is melted, about 1 to 1 1/2 hours, stirring occasionally to blend ingredients. Serve warm with taco or tortilla chips.

CHILI CHICKEN

3 whole chicken breasts (1 1/2 to 2 lbs, cut in 1 inch pieces)
1 cup chopped onion
1 cup chopped bell pepper
2 garlic cloves

2 tbsp. vegetable oil
2 cans Mexican stewed tomatoes (16 ounce each)
1 can chili beans
2/3 cup picante sauce
1 teaspoon. chili powder
1 teaspoon. cumin
1/2 teaspoon. salt

Saute chicken, onion, pepper, garlic in vegetable oil until vegetables are wilted. Transfer to slow cooker/Crock Pot and add remaining ingredients. Cook, covered, on low, for 4 to 6 hours. Serve over rice.

Serves 4 to 6.

CHILI CON QUESO
* 2 tablespoons butter
* 1 medium onion, chopped
* 1 can jalapeno peppers, chopped
* 1 15 1/2 oz. tomatoes, chopped, undrained
* 1 jar pimiento, chopped, drained
* 3/4 cup cheddar cheese, grated
* salt and pepper, to taste

Saute onion in butter in medium saucepan. Combine next 3 ingredients with onion. Heat to boiling, let simmer for 10 - 15 minutes to meld the flavors. Add cheese, mixing thoroughly until melted. Serve immediately. Note: you can add browned ground beef or sausage if you'd like; and use Velveeta instead of the cheddar cheese.

CHILI DIP
* 1 lg. jar (16oz) picante sauce, mild
* 2 cans refried beans
* 8 ounces sour cream
* 1/2 tsp. chili powder
* 1 lb. ground beef
* 1 onion, chopped
* Salt and pepper to taste
* 8 oz. Cheddar cheese, shredded
* Jalapenos or mild chile, chopped, to taste

Cook ground beef with onion; drain. Mix everything together in slow cooker/Crock Pot and cook slowly. Serve with favorite vegetables or chips.

CHOCOLATE-AMARETTO CHEESECAKE
Crust:
3/4 cup wafer-cookie or graham cracker crumbs
1/8 teaspoon almond extract
1 tablespoon sugar
3 tablespoons butter, melted
Filling:
1 cup ricotta cheese (light)
12 ounces cream cheese, light (neufchatel)
1 cup sugar
2 eggs
3 tablespoons whipping cream
1/4 cup amaretto
1/4 cup plus 1 tablespoon cocoa
1/4 cup all-purpose flour
1 teaspoon vanilla
1/3 cup semi-sweet chocolate mini-morsels
Combine crust ingredients and pat into a 7-inch springform
pan.

Beat the cheeses with the sugar until smooth; add eggs and whipping cream and beat for about 3 minutes on medium speed of an electric hand-held mixer. Add amaretto, cocoa, flour and vanilla; beat for about 1 more minute. Stir in semi-sweet chocolate morsels; pour into prepared pan. Place the cheesecake on a rack in the Crock Pot (or use a "ring" of aluminum foil to keep it off the bottom of the pot). Cover and cook on high for 2 1/2 to 3 hours. Let stand in the covered pot (after turning it off) for about 1 to 2 hours, until cool enough to handle. Cool thoroughly before removing pan sides. Chill before serving; store leftovers in the refrigerator.

CHOCOLATE BROWNIE PUDDING CAKE
1/2 cup brown sugar
3/4 cup water
2 Tbsp cocoa
2 1/2 cups brownie mix (half of a 21.5oz pkg)
1 egg
1/4 cup peanut butter

1 tablespoon soft margarine

1/4 cup water

1/4 to 1/2 cup milk chocolate chips, if desired

Combine 3/4 cup water, brown sugar, and cocoa in a saucepan. Bring to a boil. In the meantime combine the remaining ingredients in a small bowl. Whisk together or mix well with a spoon. Spread the batter evenly in the bottom of a lightly buttered slow cooker/Crock Pot. Pour boiling mixture over the batter. Cover and cook on high about 2 hours; turn heat off and let stand for about 30 minutes. I made this in a 5-quart pot, but I'm sure it would be fine in a 3 1/2- quart (I'll try that size next). Spoon into dessert dishes while warm; serve with whipped cream or ice cream.

Serves 6 to 8.

CHOCOLATE CHIP PEANUT BUTTER CAKE

1/2 cup butter

1/2 cup sugar

1/2 cup brown sugar

3 eggs, beaten

1/2 cup peanut butter

3/4 cup light sour cream

1 teaspoon vanilla extract

2 1/2 cups all-purpose flour

1 teaspoon baking powder

1 teaspoon baking soda

1/2 teaspoon salt

1 cup chocolate chips

Cream butter and sugars. Beat eggs in well. Mix in peanut butter, sour cream, and vanilla.

Combine flour, baking powder, soda and salt together and add to creamed mixture. Stir in most of the chocolate chips, reserving a few for the top. Spoon mixture into a greased and floured 2 1/2 to

3-quart souffle dish or mold (which will fit in your Crock Pot). Place a small trivet (or fashion a little "ring" from aluminum foil) in the Crock Pot, place the dish on the trivet, then cover the dish with 4 layers of paper towels. Cover loosely to allow steam to escape and cook on high for about 4 hours.

Test with a toothpick for doneness. Cool in pot until dish is cool enough to handle, then transfer to a wire rack to cool completely.

CHOCOLATE PEANUT BUTTER CAKE
2 c. chocolate cake mix
1/2 c. water
1/3 c. creamy peanut butter
1/2 c. chopped nuts

Combine all ingredients in bowl mixing well. Beat about 2 minutes. Pour batter into greased and floured 2 pound coffee can. Place can in crockpot. Cover top of can with 8 paper towels. Cover crockpot and bake on high 2 to 3 hours.

CHOPS IN A CROCK
6 pork chops, browned (you can skip the browning)
1 onion, chopped
3 T. catsup
10.5 oz can cream of mushroom soup
2 t Worcestershire sauce

Place into crockpot and simmer about 4-5 hours. Serve with rice, noodles or potatoes.

CHRISTMAS BREAD PUDDING
9 slices Whole Wheat Bread
8 slices White Bread
3 Egg Yolks, beaten
1 1/2 cups Light Cream
2/3 cup Dark Raisins
1/3 cup Whole Candied Red Cherries, halved
3/4 cup Cream Sherry
1 cup -Water
2 Egg Yolks, beaten
1/4 cup Powdered Sugar, sifted
2 tablespoons Cream Sherry
1/3 cup Sugar
dash Salt
1 1/2 teaspoons Vanilla

2/3 cup Golden raisins
1/4 teaspoon Vanilla
1/2 cup Whipping cream
Remove crusts from bread. Cover bread slices with paper towels and let stand overnight.

Custard: in a heavy medium saucepan combine three egg yolks, light cream, sugar and salt. Cook and stir over medium heat. Continue cooking until mixture coats a metal spoon. Remove from

heat; cool at once by setting saucepan in a sink of ice water and stirring for 1-2 minutes. Stir in 1 1/2 teaspoons vanilla. Cover surface with clear plastic wrap. In small bowl combine raisins. Place cherries in another bowl. Heat 3/4 cup sherry till warm. Pour 2/3 cup sherry over cherries. Set aside. Cut bread into 1/2-inch cubes (about 9 cups). In a bowl, fold bread into custard, until coated. Grease a 6 1/2 cup tower mold (without tube). Drain raisins and cherries, reserving sherry.

Arrange 1/4 of cherries in bottom of the mold, sprinkle 1/3 cup raisins into the mold. Add 1/4 of bread cube mixture. Sprinkle with 2 tablespoons reserved sherry. Repeat layers three times, arranging cherries and raisins near edges of the mold. Lightly press last layer with back of spoon. Pour remaining reserved sherry over all. Cover mold tightly with foil. Set mold in cooker - for a 5-6qt cooker, pour 1 1/2 cups water around mold (for a 3 1/2 - 4 qt cooker use 1 cup water). Cover, cook on low 5 1/2 hours or until pudding springs back when touched.

Meanwhile make the sherry sauce: in a mixing bowl combine 2 egg yolks, powdered sugar, 2 tablespoons sherry and 1/4 teaspoons vanilla. In small bowl, beat whipping cream until small peaks form. Gently fold whip cream into egg yolk mixture. Cover and chill until serving time.

Remove mold from cooker, let stand 10 minutes. Carefully unmold to serving platter. Serve warm with sherry sauce.

Serves 12.

Alternative: Remove pudding from mold, cover and chill. To serve, return pudding to same mold. Cover with foil, place in cooker. Pour 1 1/2 cup water around mold. Cover, cook on high for 1 ½ to 2 hours, or until warm. Let stand 10 minutes, unmold and serve with sauce.

CHUNK-STYLE APPLESAUCE
    8 to 10 large cooking apples, peeled, cored, and sliced or cut
in chunks
    1/2 cup water
    1 tsp cinnamon
    1/2 to 1 cup sugar
    Put ingredients in Crock-Pot. Cover; cook on Low 8 to 10
hours. (High: 3 to 4 hours.) Serve warm.
    Add cream if desired.

CINNAMON-APPLE BREAD PUDDING
    * 2 tablespoons butter
    * 2 apples, cored peeled, and chopped
    * 3/4 cup brown sugar, divided
    * 1 1/2 teaspoons cinnamon, divided
    * 2 large eggs
    * 12 oz can evaporated milk
    * 3/4 cup apple juice
    * 2 1/2 cups French bread torn in 1/2 to 1- inch pieces
    Melt butter in bottom of a 1 1/2 to 2- quart casserole or souf-
fle dish which will fit in the slow cooker/Crock Pot. Sprinkle with 2
tablespoons brown sugar and ½ teaspoon cinnamon. Add apples.
Whisk eggs, milk, and apple juice together; mix in remainder of
brown sugar, 1 teaspoon cinnamon, and the bread pieces. Place a
trivet or aluminum foil ring in the slow cooker/Crock Pot. Pour 3/4 cup
hot water into the the slow cooker/Crock Pot. Place the casserole dish
on the ring in the slow
    cooker/Crock Pot. Cover and cook on high for 2 1/2 hours, un-
til knife inserted comes out clean. Serve warm with vanilla ice cream
or sweetened whipped cream.

CITRUS FISH
    * 1 1/2 lb. fish fillets
    * Salt and pepper to taste
    * 1 med. onion, chopped
    * 5 tbsp. chopped parsley
    * 4 tsp. oil
    * 2 tsp. grated lemon rind

* 2 tsp. grated orange rind
* Orange and lemon slices

Butter slow cooker/Crock Pot and put salt and pepper on fish to taste. Then place fish in pot. Put onion, parsley and grated rinds and oil over fish. Cover and cook on low for 1 1/2 hours. Serve garnished with orange and lemon slices.

CLASSIC SWISS FONDUE
* 1 clove garlic
* 2 1/2 cups dry white Rhine, Chablis or Riesling wine
* 1 TBS lemon juice
* 1 lb. Swiss cheese, grated
* 1/2 lb. Cheddar cheese, grated
* 3 TBS flour
* 3 TBS kirsch
* Freshly ground nutmeg
* Pepper
* Paprika
* 1 loaf Italian or French bread, cut into 1-inch cubes

Rub an enameled or stainless steel pan with garlic clove. Heat wine to a slow simmer (just under boiling). Add lemon juice. Combine cheeses and flour and gradually stir in. Using a figure-8 motion, stir constantly until cheese is melted. Pour into lightly greased Crock-Pot. Add kirsch; stir well. Sprinkle with nutmeg, pepper and paprika. Cover and cook on High setting for 30 minutes, then turn to Low setting for 2 to 5 hours. Keep on Low setting while serving. Using fondue forks, dip bread cubes into fondue.

About 2 quarts

COCKTAIL KIELBASA
* 2 rings of Kielbasa (about 2 lbs)
* 1 (18 oz) jar apple jelly
* 1 (9 oz) jar prepared mustard

Slice Kielbasa 1/4 to 1/2 inch thick. Mix jelly and mustard in slow cooker/Crock Pot. Add sliced Kielbasa and mix until meat is covered. Set slow cooker/Crock Pot on low to cook for 2 hours and keep on low while serving. Stir periodically.

CONGRESSIONAL BEAN SOUP IN A CROCKPOT

1 lb Small white beans
8 c Water
2 c Ham, diced
1 c Onion, diced
1 c Celery, chopped
2 tb Parsley, chopped
1 ts Salt
1/4 ts Pepper
1 Bay leaf
Assemble ingredients in Slow Cooker. Cover and cook on low
8-10 hours or until beans are tender.

CORN CHOWDER
2 cans (16 oz) whole kernel corn, drained
2 to 3 medium potatoes, chopped
1 onion, chopped
1/2 teaspoon salt
pepper to taste
2 cups chicken broth
2 cups milk
1/4 cup butter or margarine
Combine first 6 ingredients in Crock Pot. Cover and cook on
low for 7 to 9 hours. Puree in a blender or food processor, if desired,
then return to pot. Stir in milk and butter; cook on high about 1 hour
more.
Serves 6 to 8.

COUNTRY APPLES
* 4-5 cups apples
* 2 tbsp flour
* 1/3 cup sugar
* 1/3 cup raisins
* 1/4 tsp cinnamon
* 2/3 cup oatmeal
* 3 tbsp butter
* 3/4 cup brown sugar
Peel, slice and coat apples with flour and 1/3 cup sugar. Stir in
the raisins, cinnamon, and oatmeal. Pour 1 cup water into crockery.

Add apple mix. Pour melted butter over apples and then brown sugar. Cook on Low 4-6 hours.

Serves 6.

You can serve over vanilla ice cream, use as a crepe filling or over

oatmeal for breakfast.

COUNTRY CAPTAIN CHICKEN BREASTS

The distinctive combination of curry, ginger, and fruit gives this classic Southern

dish its character.

2 medium-size Granny Smith apples

1 small onion, finely chopped

1 small green bell pepper, seeded and finely chopped

3 cloves garlic, minced or pressed

2 tablespoons dried currants

1 tablespoon curry powder

1 teaspoon ground ginger

1/4 teaspoon ground red pepper (cayenne)

1 can (about 14 1/2 oz.) diced tomatoes

6 small skinless, boneless chicken breast halves (about 1 3/4 lbs. total)

1/2 cup chicken broth

1 cup long-grain white rice

1 pound large raw shrimp, shelled and deveined

1/3 cup slivered almonds

Salt

Chopped parsley

-Quarter, core, and dice unpeeled apples. In a 4-quart or larger electric slow cooker, combine apples, onion, bell pepper, garlic, currants, curry powder, ginger, and red pepper; stir in tomatoes. Rinse chicken and pat dry; then arrange, overlapping pieces slightly, on top of tomato mixture. Pour in broth. Cover and cook at low setting until chicken is very tender when pierced (6 to 7 hours).

-Carefully lift chicken to a warm plate, cover lightly, and keep warm in a 200 degree oven. Stir rice into cooking liquid. Increase cooker heat setting to high; cover and cook, stirring once or twice, until rice is almost tender to bite (30 to 35 minutes). Stir in shrimp, cover and cook until shrimp are opaque in center; cut to test (about 10 more minutes).

-Meanwhile, toast almonds in a small nonstick frying pan over medium heat until golden brown (5 to 8 minutes), stirring occasionally. Set aside.

-To serve, season rice mixture to taste with salt. Mound in a warm serving dish; arrange chicken on top. Sprinkle with parsley and almonds.

Makes 6 servings.

CRAB DIP
* 1 lb. Velveeta cheese
* 1 lb. butter or margarine
* 2 cans crab meat

Heat together. Keep warm in fondu or slow cooker/Crock Pot. Serve with bread sticks.

CRANBERRY-APPLE TURKEY BREAST
* 2 teaspoons melted butter or margarine
* 1/2 cup chicken broth
* 1 large apple, cored and chopped
* 1/2 cup chopped onion
* 1 stalk celery, chopped
* 1 cup whole berry cranberry sauce
* 3/4 teaspoon poultry seasoning
* 2 cups seasoned crumb-style stuffing
* 2 to 3 pounds turkey breast cutlets.

Combine butter, chicken broth, apple, onion, celery, cranberry sauce, poultry seasoning and stuffing. Place 3 tablespoons stuffing mix on each turkey cutlet.

Roll up and tie. Place in stoneware. Cover; cook on LOW 8 hours (HIGH 4 hours).

CRANBERRY COCKTAIL MEATBALLS
* 2 pounds Ground beef
* 1 cup Cornflake crumbs
* 2 Eggs
* 1/2 cup Chopped, fresh parsley
* 1/3 cup Ketchup

* 3 tablespoons Minced onions
* 2 tablespoons Soy sauce
* 1/4 teaspoon Garlic powder
* 1/4 teaspoon Pepper
Sauce
* 16 ounces Can, jellied or whole cranberry sauce
* 12 ounces Chili sauce
* 1 tablespoon Brown sugar
* 1 tablespoon Lemon juice

In a large bowl, combine ground beef, cornflake crumbs, parsley, eggs, ketchup,

onion, soy sauce, garlic powder and pepper. Mix well and form into small balls, from 1/2" to 3/4" in diameter. Place in a casserole or baking pan. Heat oven to 300 degrees F. Meanwhile in a saucepan,combine cranberry sauce, chili sauce, brown sugar and lemon juice. Cook stirring over medium heat until smooth. Pour hot sauce over meatballs in casserole. Bake for 30 to 45 minutes, depending on the size of the meatballs. Transfer to Crock Pot and keep on low for serving.

CREAM CHEESE CROCKPOT CHICKEN

1 frying chicken, cut up (I used about 4 pounds of breast and rib chicken pieces)
2 tbsp melted butter
salt and pepper to taste
1 package of dry Italian seasoning mix
1 can cream of chicken soup
1 8 oz brick of cream cheese, cut up in cubes
1/2 C chicken broth
1 large onion
crushed garlic to taste

Brush chicken with butter and sprinkle with the dry Italian seasoning mix (I did two layers in my crockpot to make sure that the Italian seasoning got on all the chicken and not just those peices on top.)

Cover and cook on low for 6-7 hours. About 45 minutes before done, brown the onion in the butter and then add the cream cheese,

soup, and chicken broth to the saucepan. Add the crushed garlic and stir
all ingredients until smooth. Add salt and pepper to taste. Pour sauce mixture over chicken in crockpot and cook an additional 30-45 minutes. Remove chicken to platter and stir sauce before putting in gravy

CREAMY CHICKEN AND RICE
* chicken tenders (3 per person)
* cream of mushroom soup
(1 can for 2-3 people, 2 for 4-6)
* Mrs. Grass Onion Soup Mix (1 per each can of soup)
* 1Tbsp olive oil
* long grain brown rice (1 cup per can of soup)
* 1Tbsp whole thyme, crushed
* S&P to taste
* desired amount of broccoli florettes (optional)
* diced red pepper (optional)

When using brown rice, you need 2 1/4 cups liquid for each 1 cup rice. So I empty my can of soup into a measuring cup, and add water (or white wine) to equal 2 ½ (not a typo, you need the extra for the onion soup mix). Heat olive oil in a sauté pan, and add rice until it begins to crackle, but not brown. This will make the rice dense, and help it keep it's shape while cooking. Whisk together the soups and additional H2o, herbs and seasonings. Combine all ingredients (except veggies) in crockpot, and cook on high 4-6 hours, or 8-10 hours on low. During last 30-45 minutes, add desired veggies.
Great with crusty bread, and a fresh salad.

CREAMY CORN
2 cups corn
2 tablespoons sugar
2 eggs
1/4 cup flour
2 tablespoons butter
1 cup milk
1/2 teaspoon salt
Mix corn, sugar, eggs, flour, butter, milk and salt; place in slow cooker. Cook on high for one hour.

CREAMY ORANGE CHEESECAKE
Crust:
3/4 cup cookie or graham cracker crumbs
2 tablespoons sugar
3 tablespoons melted butter
Filling:
16 ounces cream cheese (light)
2/3 cup sugar
2 eggs
1 egg yolk
1/4 cup frozen orange juice concentrate, thawed
1 teaspoon orange or lemon zest, or dried grated rind
1 tablespoon flour
1/2 teaspoon vanilla
Combine crumbs with sugar; mix in melted butter until well moistened. Pat into a 7- inch springform pan.

In a medium bowl, cream together the cream cheese and sugar. Add eggs and yolk and beat for about 3 minutes on medium with a hand-held electric mixer. Beat in orange juice, zest, flour, and vanilla. Beat for another 2 minutes. Pour batter into prepared crust; place on a rack or aluminum foil ring in the crockery cooker (so it doesn't rest on the bottom of the pot). Cover and cook on high for 2 1/2 to 3 hours. Turn off and leave for 1 to 2 hours, until cool enough to remove. Cool completely and remove the sides of the pan. Chill before serving, and store leftovers in the refrigerator.

CREAMY SCALLOPED POTATOES (CROCKPOT)
* 3 cups Thinly sliced carrots
* 3 tablespoons Butter or margarine
* 2 cups Water
* 3 tablespoons Orange marmalade
* 1/4 teaspoon Salt
* 2 tablespoons Chopped pecans
Combine carrots, water, and salt in Crock Pot. Cover and cook on high 2 to 3 hours or until the carrots are done. Drain well; stir in remaining ingredients. Cover and cook on high 20-30 minutes.

Makes 5 to 6 servings.

CREAMY SPINACH DIP
* 8 ounces Cream cheese, cubed
* 5 ounces Frozen chopped spinach
* 2 tablespoons Pimento, diced
* 1 teaspoon Worcestershire sauce
* 1/4 teaspoon Garlic salt
* 1/4 cup Whipping ceram
* 2 tablespoons Parmesan cheese, grated
* 2 teaspoons Onion, finely chopped
* 1/2 teaspoon Thyme

Combine cream cheese and cream in Crock Pot. Cover and heat until cheese is melted, 30 to 60 minutes.

Add remaining ingredients. Cover and heat 30 minutes.

Serve with raw vegetables, crackers, or bread pieces.

CROCKED KIELBASA
1/2 pound Lean ground beef
1 pound Kielbasa sausage -- sliced
1 Can whole tomatoes -- (28 ounces) undrained
9 ounces Frozen French-cut Green beans
1 Can pitted black olives -- (6 ounces)(drained and left whole)
1/2 cup Red wine
3 Garlic cloves -- minced
1 medium Onion -- sliced
1 medium Green pepper -- chopped
1 teaspoon Basil -- crushed
1 teaspoon Oregano -- crushed
1/2 teaspoon Thyme -- crushed
1/4 teaspoon Pepper
1 pound Pasta of your choice
4 ounces Parmesan -- freshly grated

In a medium skillet, saute ground beef. When browned, transfer to crockpot. Add all other ingredients except pasta and parmesan Simmer on low for 6-8 hours. Cook pasta according to directions. Ladle Crocked Kielbasa over pasta in large bowls. Pass the Parmesan cheese to garnish.

CROCKPOT ALMOST LASAGNA

1 box rotini (or ziti), any fun, flavorful pasta will do
2 - 28-oz jars pasta sauce(one with tomato chunks works well)
1 egg
1/2 lb ground beef
1/2 lb sausage
2 tbsp olive oil
1 C. parmesan cheese
1/2 C italian breadcrumbs
1 bag mozzarella cheese
16-20 oz. ricotta cheese
2 eggs
1 C. parmesan cheese
1 1/2 tsp. parsley flakes
dash salt & pepper

Grease crock-pot, or spray with non-stick cooking spray. Cook rotini according to package directions, drain. Brown and drain meat. Toss pasta with olive oil. Add pasta sauce to mixture, toss well. Stir together parmesan cheese, breadcrumbs, egg, 1/2 bag mozzarella cheese, and browned meat. Can sprinkle lightly with garlic

powder. Beat together ricotta, 2 eggs, parmesan, parsley, salt & pepper. Pour half of pasta/sauce/meat mixture into crock-pot. Spread entire ricotta mixture over first layer of pasta. Cover ricotta layer with remaining pasta mixture, and cover with remaining cheese. Cover, and cook on low 4-6 hours.

CROCKPOT APPLE AND BROWN SUGAR CORNED BEEF

1 corned beef brisket
1 quart apple juice
1 cup brown sugar
1 Tbsp prepared mustard
8 small red potatoes
2 medium carrots, pared and cut into chunks
1 onion, peeled and cut into eights
1/2 head cabbage, cut into chunks

Place all ingredients in large crock pot (cut meat in half if necessary). Stir to mix.

Cook on high for 4 to 5 hours on high or 8 to 10 hours on low. Remove meat and vegetables and some of the cooking liquid. Slice meat thinly across the grain.

Serve with the vegetables and some of the liquid.

Use left over corn beef the next day.....layer in crock pot with sauerkraut and swiss cheese. Warm and serve on rye bread with 1000 Island dressing!

CROCKPOT APPLE BROWN BETTY

3 lbs. cooking apples
10 slices of bread, cubed (about 4 cups)
1/2 tsp. cinnamon
1/4 tsp. nutmeg
1/8 tsp. salt
3/4 c. brown sugar
1/2 c. butter or margarine, melted

Wash apples, peel, core, cut into eighths; place in bottom on crock. Combine bread cubes, cinnamon, nutmeg, salt, sugar, butter; toss together. Place on top of apples in crock. Cover. Place crock into outer shell. Cook on low setting 2 to 4 hours.

Makes 6 to 8 servings.

CROCKPOT APPLE BUTTER I

apples -- cut up, to fill 3 1/2 qt. crockpot
1 cup brown sugar
1 cup apple cider
juice of 1 lemon
1 tablespoon cinnamon

Cut blemishes off apples and cut into chunks to fill 3 1/2 qt. crockpot. Add sugar, cider and lemon juice. Cover and cook on Low for 8 hours. Stir. Add cinnamon and cook another 10 hours. Stir occasionally until brown. Run through Food mill or any strainer to strain out seeds and skins. I used the blender. To thicken, if not thick enough, return to slow cooker and cook on High uncovered until desired consistency.

YIELD: Makes 3-4 pints.

CROCKPOT APPLE BUTTER II

Peel and core apples, cut in quarters, enough to fill a 4 quart crockpot to about 1

1/2 inches from the top:

ADD:

4 tsp. Cinnamon

1/2 tsp Cloves

1/2 tsp Salt

3 Cups Sugar

Start on high with about 4 TB water, til it gets hot, then turn on low and cook all day. When it is done and apples are fully cooked down put small amounts into food processor and zap quickly till smooth.

NOTE: If you are canning this, put into jars and seal while "HOT".

CROCKPOT APPLE BUTTER III

4 lbs apples, cored and sliced (don't peel)

1 1/3 cups packed brown sugar

1 cup apple cider

grated zest and juice of one lemon

3 TBS grated ginger

Combine apples, brown sugar, apple cider, zest, juice. Cover and cook 8-10 hours on low, til apples are very soft. (A good thing to do overnight!) Then stir in ginger, increase heat to high, uncover and cook (stirring now and then) til mixture is reduced to about 3 cups for 8 to 10 hours. (This part sounds kind of incredible, come to think of it...I can't imagine sticking around for 10 hours to stir occasionally...oh well, I've come this far, might as well continue!). Put the resulting mash through a food mill.

CROCKPOT APPLE BUTTER IV

2 qt. sweet cider

4lbs apples, peeled, cored & sliced

3 C. sugar

1/4 tsp. cinnamon

1/4 tsp. allspice

1/8 tsp. cloves
1 tsp. salt
Place apples & cider in crock pot. Cover & cook on LOW 10 - 12 hrs. DO NOT STIR!!!!!!! Put apples through a srine (a fine mesh strainer works well too). Mash apples. Add equal parts sugar stirring well between each, add spices & salt STIR WELL!! Return to crockpot. Cook on HIGH 1 hr. Pour into 1/2 pint jars, seal and process 10 min. If you don't want to process keep it refrigerated! makes 5 half pints.

CROCKPOT APPLE CAKE DESSERT
6 apples peeled, cored and sliced
sugar
cinnamon
8 oz of yellow cake mix
1/4 c melted butter or margarine
Put slices of apples in CP. Pour half a package of dry cake mix over apples.
Drizzle butter over cake mix. Sprinkle cinnamon and sugar mixture over that and cook on low 1 1/2 to 2 hours. Keep checking and it's done when the apples are soft.

CROCKPOT APPLE CARAMEL DESSERT
2 med apple
1/2 c apple juice
7 oz caramel candy
1 tsp vanilla
1/8 tsp ground cardamom
1/2 tsp ground cinnamon
1/3 c peanut butter, creamy
7 slices angel food cake
1 qt vanilla ice cream
Peel, core and cut each aplle into 18 wedges; set aside. Combine apple juice, unwrapped caramel candies, vanilla, cardamom and cinnamon. Drop peanut butter, 1 tsp at a time, over ingredients in crock pot and stir. Add apple wedges; cover and cook on LOW for 5 hrs. Stir thoroughly, then cook 1 hr more. Serve approx 1/3 cup

of warm mixture over a slice of angel food cake or ice cream.

CROCKPOT APPLE CIDER

1 gallon of apple cider

Put it in a crock pot. Add 3 cinnamon sticks, about a tsp of whole cloves, and about 3 or 4 whole allspice. Slice up an orange and put orange rings in there. Put it on low and let it simmer all day. It's easier if you can put the spices in cheese cloth but I don't always have that. Also, taste it after about 4 or 5 hours to make sure it's not getting too strong. Remove the spices and oranges when the flavor reaches the taste you prefer.

CROCKPOT APPLE COCONUT CRISPS

4 large Granny Smith apples, peeled & coarsely sliced (about 4 cups)

1/2 cup sweetened flaked coconut

1 tablespoon flour

1/3 cup brown sugar

1/2 cup butterscotch or caramel ice cream topping (fat-free is fine)

1/2 teaspoon cinnamon

1/3 cup flour

1/2 cup quick rolled oats

2 tablespoons butter or margarine

In a casserole 1 1/2-quart baking dish that fits in the crockpot, combine apples with coconut, 1 tablespoon flour, 1/3 cup brown sugar, and cinnamon. Drizzle with the ice cream topping. Combine remaining ingredients in a small bowl with a fork or pastry cutter and sprinkle over apple mixture. Cover and cook on high for 2 1/2 to 3 hours, until apples are tender. Serve warm with vanilla ice cream or whipped topping.

CROCKPOT APPLE DESSERT I

6 apples, peeled and sliced

2/3 cup raw oatmeal

2/3 cup sugar

1/3 cup flour
1 tsp cinnamon
1/4 tsp nutmeg
1/4 tsp ginger
1/3 cup butter or margarine, melted

Mix oatmeal, sugar, flour, and spices in small bowl. Stir melted butter into mixture until it is crumbly. Put about half of sliced apples in crockpot and spoon about half of oatmeal mixture on top. Cover with the rest of the apples and top with the rest of the crumbly mixture. Cook on high about 2 1/2 hours.

CROCKPOT APPLE DESSERT II

2 Cups milk
1/4 cup brown sugar
1 tbsp melted butter
1/4 tsp salt
1/2 tsp cinnamon
1 cup rolled oats, regular
1 cup chopped apples
1/2 cup raisons

Spray or butter inside of crock pot. add ingredients to pot and stir cover and cook on low overnight.

CROCKPOT APPLE PIE

8 Tart Apples peeled and sliced
1 1/4 t ground cinnamon
1/4 t allspice
1/4 t nutmeg
3/4 cup milk
2 T butter soften
3/4 c sugar
2 eggs
1 t vanilla
1/2 c Bisquick
1 c Bisquick
1/3 c brown sugar

3 T cold butter

Toss apples in large bowl with cinnamon, allspice, and nutmeg. Place in lightly greased crockpot. Combine milk, softened butter, sugar, eggs, vanilla, and the 1/2 c Bisquick. Spoon over apples.

Combine the 1 cup Bisquick and brown sugar. Cut the cold butter into mixture until crumbly. Sprinkle this mixture over top of apple mixture.

Cover and cook on low 6-7 hours or until apples are soft.

CROCKPOT APPLE SAUCE
About 3 pounds apples, peeled, cored, and sliced
1/3 cup sugar
1 cinnamon stick
2 TBS lemon juice
nutmeg

Put apples in cooker, sprinkle w/sugar and add cinnamon stick. Sprinkle lemon juice on. Cover and cook on low for 6 1/2 to 8 hours til apples form a thick sauce.

Sprinkle with nutmeg to taste.

CROCKPOT ARROZ CON POLLO
4 Chicken breast halves, skin and excess fat removed
1/4 teaspoon salt
1/4 teaspon pepper
1/4 teaspoon paprika
1 tablespoon oil
1 medium onion, chopped
1 small red pepper, chopped
1 clove of garlic, minced
1/2 teaspoon dried rosemary leaves
1 14 1/2 ounce can crushed tomatoes
1 10 oz package frozen peas

Season chicken with salt, pepper, and paprika. In a medium skillet, heat oil over medium-high heat. Add chicken and brown. Put chicken in the Crock-pot. In a small bowl, combine remaining ingredients except the peas. Pour over chicken. Cover: cook on Low 7-9 hours (High 3-4 hours) One hour before serving, add peas.

    Serve over rice.

    Makes 4 servings.

CROCKPOT ARTICHOKE, CHICKEN AND OLIVES

    1 1/2 lbs skinless, boneless chicken breast halves and/or thighs

    2 c sliced fresh mushrooms

    1 (14.5 oz) can diced tomatoes

    1 (8 or 9 oz) pkg frozen artichokes

    1 c chicken broth

    1 med onion, chopped

    1/2 c sliced pitted ripe olives (or 1/4 cup capers, drained)

    1/4 c dry white wine or chicken broth

    3 tbsp quick cooking tapioca

    2-3 tsp curry powder

    3/4 tsp dried thyme, crushed

    1/4 tsp salt

    1/4 tsp pepper

    4 c hot cooked couscous

    Rinse chicken & set aside. In a 3 1/2 qt crock pot combine mushrooms, undrained

tomatoes, frozen artichoke hearts, chicken broth, onion, olives, & wine/broth. Stir in tapioca, curry powder, thyme, salt, & pepper. Add chicken. Spoon some of the tomato mixture over chicken. Cover & cook on LOW for 7 to 8 hours or on HIGH for 3 1/2 to 4 hours. Serve with hot cooked couscous. Serves 6.

    Per serving - 345 calories, 6g total fat (1g saturated fat), 60mg cholesterol, 531 mg sodium, 43g carbohydrate (with couscous?), 9g fiber, 30g protein

CROCKPOT ARTICHOKES

    5 artichokes, remove stalks and tough leaves

    1 1/2 ts salt

    8 peppercorns

2 stalks celery, cut up
1/2 lemon, sliced
2 c boiling water
Combine all ingredients in crockpot. Cook on High 4 - 5 hours.

CROCKPOT AUTUMN CHICKEN

2 large or 4 small chicken breasts
2 parsnips - 2 carrots
1 acorn squash
1 14.5 oz. can of chicken broth
garlic
salt
pepper
nutmeg
honey

Peel and chop carrots and parsnips and place them in the bottom of the crockpot.

Sprinkle with garlic (I used a teaspoon of pre-chopped garlic. I'm not sure how many cloves of fresh garlic that would be.) Place chicken on top. Pour in broth.

Cut squash into chunks and slice off the skin. Place on top of chicken. Sprinkle desired amounts of salt, pepper and nutmeg on top of squash and drizzle enough honey on top to lightly cover the squash. Cook on low 8-10 hours.

CROCKPOT AUTUMN PORK CHOPS

Serving Size : 6
6 pork chops
2 medium acorn squash -- unpeeled
3/4 teaspoon salt
2 tablespoons melted butter
3/4 cup brown sugar -- packed
3/4 teaspoon brown bouquet sauce
1 tablespoon orange juice
1/2 teaspoon orange peel -- grated

-Trim excess fat from chops. Cut each squash into 4 to 5 crosswise slices; remove seeds.

-Arrange 3 chops on bottom of slow-cooking pot.

-Place all squash slices on top; then another layer of remaining 3 chops.

-Combine salt, butter, sugar, bouquet sauce, orange juice, and orange peel. Spoon
over chops.

-Cover and cook on low for 4 to 6 hours or until done.

-Serve one or two slices of squash with each pork chop.

CROCKPOT AUTUMN PORK ROAST
3 to 4 lb. pork roast
Salt & pepper
1 c. cranberries, finely chopped
1/4 c. honey
1 tsp. grated orange peel
1/8 tsp. ground cloves
1/8 tsp. ground nutmeg

-Sprinkle roast with salt and pepper. Place in slow cooking crockpot.

-Combine remaining ingredients. Pour over roast. Cover. Cook on low for 8 to 10
hours. or on High for 4-5 .Makes 6 to 8 servings.

CROCKPOT AZTEC BLACK BEANS
1 lb. dried black beans (or turtle beans)
16 oz. jar of salsa (your favorite kind)

-Rinse black beans, removing any stones or foreign objects. Cover with water, soak
all night.

-Drain beans and place in cp with salsa. Add enough water to just cover beans.

Cover and cook on low 8-10 hours.

CROCKPOT BAKED APPLES
2 tbsp raisins
1/4 cup sugar
6 to 8 apples, washed and cored
1 tsp cinnamon

2 tbsp butter

Mix raisins and sugar, fill center of apples. Sprinkle with cinnamon and dot with butter. Put in crockpot; add 1/2 cup water. Cover; cook on Low 7 to 9 hours.

CROCKPOT BAKED BEANS I

1 pound dried small white beans -- rinsed
4 1/2 cups water
1/3 cup molasses
1/4 cup brown sugar
1 onion -- chopped
1/4 pound salt pork -- cut into 1" cubes
1 tablespoon dijon-style mustard
1/2 teaspoon salt

In slow-cooker, combine all ingredients. Cover and cook on LOW 13 to 14 hours, stirring occasionally, if possible.

CROCKPOT BAKED BEANS II

1 lb ground beef
3/4 lb bacon fried and diced
1 onion lg chopped and browned
1 lge can pork and beans
1 16 oz kidney beans canned
1 16 oz buttered lima beans canned
1 cup catsup
3 Tbsp white vinegar
1/4 cup liquid smoke
1 tsp salt
dash pepper
Directions:

Put all ingre. in crock pot cook 4-6 hrs on low. The longer you cook it the better it will taste.

CROCKPOT BAKED BEANS III

2 cans canellini beans
2 cans black beans

2 cans red kidney beans
1 can chick peas
2 diced onions
2 tablespoons mustard (from the fridge - the wet kind)
1 cup molasses
1/2 cup brown sugar
3/4 cup maple syrup
Rinse and drain beans and set aside.

On bottom of crockpot place diced onions, then dump on beans (don't mix just dump
'em all on). Then drizzle on all other ingredients. Mustard stays lumpy - it's ok.

If you wish to add bacon - pre cook 1 lb. crumble and put over top of entire
mixture.

DON'T STIR. It will look dry for awhile. Crock Pot on High for 6-8 hours (I do 5-6)
stirring once about 3/4 of the way through.
Serve. Enjoy!!

CROCKPOT BAKED BEANS IV

24 to 32 oz. canned Pork and Beans, undrained
3/4 cup firmly packed brown sugar-I use light rather than dark
1 cup ketchup
1 large onion, diced
1 tsp. prepared mustard
2 to 3 slices bacon

Combine all ingredients in CP. Cover and cook on low about 6 hours. If you prefer, can be baked in oven. Use a greased 2qt casserole. Put bacon on top and bake at 350°F 1 1/2 hours. The CP version is soupier.

CROCKPOT BARBECUED SHORT RIBS

2 c. water
3 or 4 lbs. boneless short ribs
18 oz. bottle barbecue sauce
1 tbsp. Worcestershire sauce
3 oz. Heinz 57 hickory smoke sauce

1/4 tsp. angostura

1/4 tbsp. lemon pepper seasoning

Combine water, barbecue sauce, Worcestershire, Heinz 57 sauce, angostura, lemon pepper and short ribs in crock pot on low heat for 12 hours. I usually cook this recipe overnight.

CROCKPOT BEANS

1 lb. ground beef

3/4 lb. fried crumbled bacon

1 c. chopped onions

1 c. ketchup

1/4 c. brown sugar

1/2 tsp. pepper

1 tsp. hickory smoke flavoring

1 lb. can each pork and beans, lima beans, butter beans, and kidney beans

-Cook on low in crockpot for 4-8 hours. The longer it cooks, the smokier it tastes.

CROCKPOT BEEF AND BEANS

1 1/2 lbs of stewing beef

1 tbsp. prepared mustard

1 tbsp. taco seasoning

1/2 tsp. salt

1/4 tsp. pepper

2 garlic cloves minced

1 can 16 oz diced tomatoes, undrained

1 med. onion chopped

1 can Kidney beans rinsed and drained

1 can chili beans

(I also added 1 can of black beans)

-Combine mustard, taco seasonings, salt , pepper and garlic in a large bowl. Add beef and toss to coat!

-Put the beef in your crock pot and add the rest of the ingriedients. Cover and cook for 6 -8 hours on LOW.

-Serve over yummy hot rice!

CROCKPOT BEEF AND CHIPOTLE BURRITOS

1 1/2 lb. boneless beef round steak, cut 3/4" thick

1 14 1/2 oz. can diced tomatoes

1 sm. onion, chopped

1 to 2 canned chipotle peppers in adobo sauce, chopped (my local stores didn't carry this - of course- so I substituted a jar of salsa with chipolte, I think it was Old El Paso or Pace)

1 tsp. dried oregano, crushed

1/4 tsp. ground cumin

1 clove garlic, minced

6 9-10" tomato-flavored or plain flour tortillas, warmed

3/4 c. shredded sharp cheddar cheese (3 oz.)

1 recipe Pico de Gallo Salsa (we're talking real life here - I substituted a small jar of regular salsa :) Shredded jicama or radishes (optional, VERY optional!)

Dairy sour cream (optional)

Directions: Trim fat from meat. Cut meat into 6 pieces. In a 3 1/2 or 4 qt. crockery cooker place meat, undrained tomatoes, onion, peppers, oregano, cumin, and garlic.

Cover; cook on low-heat setting for 8 to 10 hours or on high-heat setting for 4 to 5 hours. Remove meat from cooker. Using 2 forks, shred meat. Spoon one-sixth of the meat onto each warm tortilla just below the center. Top with cheese, Pico de Gallo Salsa, and if desired, jicama or radishes and sour cream. Roll up tortilla. Makes 6

servings * Prep time: 20 min.

Pico de Gallo Salsa: Combine 2 medium finely chopped tomatoes; 2 tbsp. Finely chopped onion; 2 tbsp. snipped cilantro; 1 serrano pepper; finely chopped; and dash sugar. Cover; chill several hours.

CROCKPOT BEEF AND GRAVY

2-3 pounds roast cut into bite sized pieces

1 packet Lipton's Onion soup mix

2 cans Cream of mushroom soup

Place pieces of roast in crock pot. Sprinkle packet of onion soup on meat. Cover with cream of mushroom soup. Let cook up to 9 hours. Stir about 1/2 way through cooking (but I'm sure you could just stir at the end). Serve over mashed potatoes or pasta.

CROCKPOT BEEF BOURGUIGNON I
        1 Cup Dry red wine
        2 Tablespoons Olive oil
        1 Large Onion -- sliced
        1/2 Teaspoon Thyme
        2 Tablespoons Parsley -- chopped
        1 Bay leaf
        1/4 Teaspoon Pepper
        2 Pounds stewing beef, cut into 1 1/2-inch cubes
        3 Slices Bacon (thick-cut is possible) -- diced
        12 Small White onions
        1/2 Pound Sliced mushrooms
        2 Cloves Garlic -- minced
        1 Teaspoon Salt
Combine first seven ingredients, mix well, add beef. Marinate at least 3 hours (overnight if refrigerated) Drain meat, reserving marinade. In skillet, saute bacon and remove. Brown meat in bacon fat. Combine beef, bacon, vegetables and seasonings in slow cooker. Pour over enough marinade to cover. Cook on low 8-10 hours.

CROCKPOT BEEF BOURGUIGNON II
        1 lb. bacon, cooked, reserve grease
        3 lbs. beef, cubed
        1 bottle red wine
        1 lb. onion, chopped
        1 lb. celery
        1 lb. carrots, chopped
        2 cloves garlic, chopped
        Chopped shallots (optional)
        1 bay leaf
        Salt & pepper
        Flour
Slowly cook bacon in large baking pan; remove. Dredge beef cubes in flour, brown in bacon fat. Transfer meat from skillet to heated platter. Saute vegetable and garlic in bacon fat; remove. Drain fat from pan. Gently combine beef, vegetables, bacon and half the wine. Add bay leaf and salt and pepper to taste. Cook on low 8 – 10 hours.

CROCKPOT BEEF BURGER STROGANOFF
1 1/2 lbs lean ground beef
3 slices bacon, diced
1 small onion, chopped
2 tbs flour
1/4 tsp paprika
1 tsp salt
1 can (10 3/4oz) condensed cream of mushroom soup
2 tbs dry red wine
1 cup dairy sour cream
6 to 8 hamburger buns, toasted and buttered

In large skillet, brown beef and bacon until red color disappears. Drain. In crockpot, mix together drained beef, bacon, onion, flour, paprika, and salt. Stir in undiluted soup and wine. Cover pot and cook on low 4 to 5 hours. Stir in sour cream. Spoon mixture over toasted buns. Serves 6 to 8.

I served this over buttered noodles instead of the buns.

CROCKPOT BEEF BURGUNDY I
2 slices bacon -- chopped
2 pounds sirloin tip or round steak -- cut in 1 inch cubes
1/4 cup flour
1 teaspoon salt
1/2 teaspoon seasoned salt
1/4 teaspoon marjoram
1/4 teaspoon thyme
1/4 teaspoon pepper
1 clove garlic -- minced
1 cube beef bouillon -- crushed
1 cup Burgundy wine
2 tablespoons cornstarch

In large skillet cook bacon several minutes. Remove bacon and set aside. Coat beef with flour and brown on all sides in bacon mixture. Combine steak, bacon drippings, cooked bacon, seasonings, bouillon and Burgundy in crock pot. Cover and cook on low for 6 to 8 hours or until meat is tender. Turn control to high. Add cornstarch (dissolved in 2 tablespoons water); cook on high 15 minutes. Serves 6.

NOTES : Can add 1/4 pound fresh mushrooms during last 15 minutes, if desired.

CROCKPOT BEEF BURGUNDY II

3 lbs beef, cut in large cubes-can use stew beef or round steak

1 can Minestrone Soup
1 can Tomato Bisque Soup
1 can Cream of Mushroom soup
1 envelope dry onion soup mix
1 soup can Burgundy wine

Flour and brown meat. Place in crockpot. Mix remaining ingredients and pour over meat. Cook on low 6-8 hours. Serve over noodles or rice. You could cook the rice at home and reheat in the micro at work.

CROCKPOT BEEF FAJITAS

1 1/2 pounds beef flank steak
1 cup chopped onion
1 green sweet pepper, cut into 1/2 inch pieces
1 jalapeno pepper, chopped
1 Tbsp. cilantro
2 garlic cloves, minced (or 1/4 tsp. garlic powder)
1 tsp. chili powder
1 tsp. ground cumin
1 tsp. ground coriander
1/2 tsp. salt
1 can (8oz) chopped tomatoes
12 8inch flour tortillas

Toppings: sour cream, guacamole, shredded cheddar cheese and salsa

Cut flank steak into 6 portions. In any size crockpot combine meat, onion, green pepper, jalapeno pepper, cilantro, garlic, chili powder, cumin, coriander and salt. Add tomatoes. Cover and cook on low 8-10 hours or high 4-5 hours. Remove meat from crockpot and shred. Return meat to crockpot and stir. To serve, spread meat mixture into flour tortillas and top with toppings. Roll up.

CROCKPOT BEEF FOR SANDWICHES
    1 roast
    1 packet Italian dressing mix or Ranch dressing mix OR 2 packages onion soup mix
    1 cup water
    Place all in crockpot, cook on low 8 hours.
    I used Zesty Italian dressing mix and I added 1 onion slivered up. I put it all in the crockpot the night before I was going to spend all day cooking. By morning, it was tender. I took it out shredded it and had 2 meals in the freezer by 8:30 that morning! WOO HOO It sounded almost too easy to me. But this was one of the best smelling recipes I've made in a long time! I keep hoagie buns in the freezer from
    the bread store (day old, got 'em for 2 packages for $1!!!) I'll take a pack of those out, add the beef and a slice of cheese and VOILA! Dinner!

CROCKPOT BEEF N BREW VEGETABLE SOUP
    3 medium onions, sliced
    1 lb carrots, cut into 1/2" slices
    4 parsnips, cut into 1/2" slices
    2 bay leaves
    4 cloves garlic, minced
    1 TBS snipped fresh thyme or 1 tsp dried thyme, crushed
    1/2 tsp pepper
    2 TBS quick cooking tapioca
    1 1/2 lbs beef stew meat, cut into 1" cubes
    1 14 1/2 oz can beef broth
    1 12 oz can beer
    In a 5 or 6 quart crockpot, place onions, carrots, parsnips, garlic, bay leaves, dried thyme, and pepper. Sprinkle with tapioca. Place meat on top of vegetables.
    Add beef broth and beer.
    Cover; cook on low-heat setting for 10 to 12 hours or on high-heat setting for 5 to 6 hours. To serve, remove bay leaves; if using

fresh thyme, stir in now.

CROCKPOT BEEF POT ROAST
1 1/2 lb- 2lb. pot roast meat
1 dry package of Good Seasons Garlic Dressing
1 dry pkg of Italian (or Zesty Italian) Dressing
1 can of beer (your choice-not dark)
Place one envelope of Good seasons in bottom of crock pot. Place meat on top, top with other package of dressing and pour beer over all. Let cook 8-10 hours on low. If your a gravy maker, the sauce made into a gravy is YUMMY! I serve this with potatoes.

CROCKPOT BEEF STEW I
2 lbs. stew beef
1/4 c. flour
1 tsp. paprika
4 lg. carrots
3 lg. potatoes
1 c. condensed beef broth
1 1/2 tsp. salt
1/2 tsp. pepper
1/3 c. soy sauce
1 lg. onion
1 can tomato sauce (8 oz.)
Layer potatoes, then carrots. Top with meat; sprinkle meat with soy sauce, salt, paprika, pepper & flour.
Spread with chopped onions. Combine beef broth & tomato sauce & pour overall. Cover & cook on low 7 - 8 hrs. or high 4 - 5 hrs.
NOTES:
Instead of sprinkling the meat with soy sauce, salt, paprika, pepper & flour as the recipes says, I mix those all together in a small bowl. This prevents the flour from becoming clumpy.
-Instead of chopped onions, I use 3 or 4 small yellow onions whole (I'm not an onion fan but still like the taste they give the stew.)
-I add about 1/4 cup barbecue sauce to the top, before putting the cover on. I use whatever variety of sauce that I have on hand. I don't usually buy the "regular"

flavor of any brand, but instead have hickory, brown sugar or garlic and onion

flavors. The BBQ sauce adds an extra "kick" to the meat and gravy.

-For the beef broth, since I don't usually keep that on hand, I dissolve 1 beef bouillon cube into 1 cup boiling water.

CROCKPOT BEEF STEW II

1 lb. beef bourguignon (or cheaper cut)

3 large sweet potatoes (cut into 1" thick slices)

2 cans beef bouillon (or broth or consommée)

2 small cans tomato paste

3-4 handfulls of assorted veggies (I used frozen green & yellow beans and carrots)

1 lb. fresh mushrooms (quartered)

1 large onion (diced)

2 cloves garlic (minced)

1/4 cup flour

Mix bite sized pieces of meat in flour, brown in some oil along with the diced garlic.

While meat is browning, combine beef bouillon & tomato paste in a crock pot, mix well.

Pre-cook the sweet potatoes until just tender, add to crock pot along with onions and any raw veggies that you may use. Add enough water to cover and cook on low for as long as you want, (I let it cook for about 5 hours.

I added the frozen veggies and some quartered mushrooms for about the last 1 hour or so.

I thickened it with a bit of flour and water, let it cook another 15 minutes uncovered and that was it.

CROCKPOT BEEF STEW III

1 package stew beef

1 can cream of potato soup

1 can cream of mushroom soup

1 - 1 1/2 cans of water

Cook on high all day (7-8) hours

I serve over white rice.

CROCKPOT BEEF STROGANOFF I
2 lbs top round steak, sliced thin across the grain
1 lb fresh mushrooms, sliced
1 medium onion, sliced
1/4 tsp thyme
3/4 cup dry sherry
3/4 cup beef broth (Swansons)
3/4 tsp dry mustard
1/4 tsp garlic salt
Put all this in the crockpot, stir well and cook on low for 8 hours. Turn heat to high and mix 1-1/2 cup sour cream 1/2 cup Wondra flour, cake flour works too, heat on high for 40 minutes.
Serve over rice or noodles.

CROCKPOT BEEF STROGANOFF II
1 1/2 lb. lean ground beef
1 medium onion, chopped
1 clove garlic, minced
3 Tbsp. tomato paste
1/2 c. beef broth
3 Tbsp. sherry
1 tsp. salt
Dash pepper
1 can mushrooms, drained
1 c. sour cream
Brown ground beef with onion and garlic; drain. Add to crock pot with remaining ingredients except for sour cream. Cover and cook on low for 5 to 7 hours. Stir in sour cream. Heat through. Serve over egg noodles.

CROCKPOT BEEF STROGANOFF III
3 lb. beef round steak, 1/2 inch thick
1/2 c. flour
2 tsp. salt

1/8 tsp. pepper
1/2 tsp. dry mustard
2 med. onions, thinly sliced and separated into rings
2 (4 oz. each) cans sliced mushrooms, drained or 1/2 lb. mushrooms, sliced
1 (10 1/2 oz.) can condensed beef broth
1/4 c. dry white wine (optional)
1 1/2 c. sour cream
1/4 c. flour
Trim all excess fat from steak and cut meat into 3 inch strips about 1/2 inch wide.

Combine 1/2 cup flour, the salt, pepper and dry mustard; toss with steak strips to coat thoroughly. Place coated steak strips in crock pot; stir in onion rings and mushrooms. Add beef broth and wine; stir well. Cover and cook on low setting for 8- 10 hours. Before serving, combine sour cream with 1/4 cup flour; stir into crock pot. Serve stroganoff over rice or noodles.

CROCKPOT BEEF STROGANOFF IV

1 can cream of mushroom soup
1 package onion soup mix
1 package mushroom
1 onion cut in rings
1 package beef stew meat
salt
pepper
Put in crock pot and cook all day.
Add 16 oz sour cream before serving.
Serve over Egg Noodles.

CROCKPOT BEEF TACO BEAN SOUP

2 lbs. rump roast
1 pk taco seasoning
1 can Mexican style diced tomatoes (15 oz.)
1 small can green chiles
1 can tomato sauce (8 oz)
1 onion - chopped

2 beef bouillon cubes
2 cans red kidney beans, (15 oz. each), rinsed, drained
Shredded cheddar cheese

Cut roast into bite sized chunks. Roll in taco seasoning and add to crock pot. Then add the tomatoes, chiles, tomato sauce, onion, and bouillon cubes. Cover and cook on LOW 6 hours or until meat is tender.

Add the drained beans and cook until the beans are heated through; around 30 minutes. Serve topped with cheese, and/or the toppings that you like.

CROCKPOT BEEF TIPS

1/2 c Flour
1 ts Salt
1/8 ts Pepper
4 lb Beef or sirloin tips
1/2 c Chopped green onions
2 c Sliced mushrooms (4 oz. can, drained) OR
1/2 lb Mushrooms, sliced
1 cn Condensed beef broth, (10 1/2 oz.)
1 ts Worcestershire sauce
2 ts Tomato paste or ketchup
1/4 c Dry red wine or water
3 tb Flour
1 Buttered noodles

Combine 1/2 cup flour with the salt and pepper and toss with beef cubes to coat thoroughly. Place in crock-pot. Add green onions and drained mushrooms. Combine with beef broth, Worcestershire sauce and tomato paste or ketchup. Pour over beef and vegetables; stir well. Cover and cook on LOW setting for 7 to 12 hours. One hour before serving, turn to HIGH setting. Make a smooth paste of red wine and 3

tablespoons flour; stir into crock-pot, mixing well.

CROCKPOT BEST PORK ROAST

4-5 pound pork roast
6-8 cloves garlic
pepper

basil
1 c dry white wine
onion
Cut 6-8 holes into the roast just big enough to fit a clove of
garlic. Put a garlic
clove (peeled) into each hole. Rub outside with cracked pepper and basil. Pour dry white wine in the bottom of the Crock Pot.
Place roast in the CP put slices or wedges of onion on top and around
the roast. Cover and cook on low all day or until done.

If desired you can also place potatoes and carrots in the bottom of the CP, but I usually serve either mashed or baked potatoes
and a steamed veggie on the side.

Don't forget a nice fresh loaf of bread to go with it too :)

CROCKPOT BLACK BEAN CHILI
3/4 cup cooked black beans
1 lb. stew beef, cubed
3 tablespoons oil
1/4 cup chopped onion
1/4 cup chopped green peppers
1/2 cup diced green chilies
3 tbsp. tomato paste
3 to 4 beef bouillon cubes, or beef base
1/4 tsp. ground cumin
1 tsp. minced garlic
1/2 tsp. salt and pepper
1 cup shredded Monterey Jack OR cheddar cheese
Brown stew beef in oil with onion and green pepper. Combine
all ingredients except cheese and cook 6 to 8 hours on low. Sprinkle
cheese over individual servings.

CROCKPOT BLACK BEAN CHILI WITH PORK
1 lb. boneless pork, cut into cubes
2 (16 oz.) cans black beans, drained
1 red or yellow bell pepper, chopped
1 med. tomato, peeled, seeded and chopped
1 sm. red onion, thinly sliced
1 clove garlic, crushed

1/2 t. ground cumin
2 t. chili powder
1/2 t. salt
1 can tomato sauce
1/2 c. sour cream
2 T. chopped cilantro

In a crockpot, stir together pork, beans, bell pepper, tomato, onion, garlic, cumin, chili powder, salt, and tomato sauce. Cover and cook on low 8 to 9 hours. Spoon into bowls and top with sour cream and cilantro.

CROCKPOT BLACK BEAN SOUP

2 cans, 15 oz. each, black beans, drained and rinsed
2 cans,4.5 oz, each, chopped green chiles
1 can, 14.5 oz,Mexican Stewed tomatoes, undrained
1 can,14.5 oz, diced tomatoes, undrained
1 can,11 oz, whole kernel corn, drained (I used a 16 oz can)
4 green onions, sliced
2 to 3 T. chili powder
1 tsp. ground cumin (I omitted this)
1/2 tsp. dried minced garlic

Combine all ingredients in a 5 qt. slow cooker-I think it will fit in a 3 qt, tho. Cover and cook on high 5 to 6 hours. Makes 8 cups. You can cook it low all day.

Serve it with shredded cheddar and fat free sour cream.

CROCKPOT BLACK EYED PEAS

1 16 oz bag of dried black-eyed peas
1 small ham hock
1 14 1/2 oz can of diced tomatoes with jalapenos
1 14 1/2 oz can of diced tomatoes with mild green chiles
2 10 1/2 oz cans of chicken broth
1 stalk of celery, chopped
salt and pepper to taste (it doesn't need much, if any)

Pre-soak black-eyed peas according to the instructions on the bag. Combine all ingredients and cook on low for 8-10 hours.

Serve on New Year's Day for good luck!

CROCKPOT BLACK EYED PEAS AND OKRA

2 (16 oz each) packages frozen Black Eyed peas
2 cups water
1 (15 oz) can Ranch Style Beans with Jalapenos undrained
1 cup chopped onion
1 cup chopped green pepper
1 cup chopped celery
1 (12 to 16 oz)package frozen sliced okra
1 can Ro Tel tomatoes and Green chiles

Dump all ingredients in Crock Pot. Cook on low 8 to 10 hours. May take even longer.

I start mine on high for several hours, then switch to low for the remaining time.

VARIATION: Substitute 4 (15oz) cans of canned Black Eyed peas (undrained) and omit the water.

CROCKPOT BONELESS TWICE COOKED BBQ RIBS

Throw about 1 1/2 lbs of boneless ribs in the CP on low with enough water to cover, about 3 TBS of BBQ sauce, fresh chopped garlic, 1/3 CUP brown sugar and a couple dashes of ketchup. Cook on low about 5 hours until done. Throw on the BBQ to crisp them up and baste with more BBQ sauce.

CROCKPOT BOSTON BAKED BEANS

1 lb small dry white beans
1 medium onion, chopped
4 slices bacon, chopped
1/4 cup light (mild) molasses
1/4 cup packed dark brown sugar
2 teaspoons dry mustard
1/4 teaspoon ground black pepper
1/8 teaspoon ground cloves
1 1/2 teaspoons salt

-Rinse beans with cold running water and discard any stones or shriveled beans. In a large bowl, place beans and enough water to cover by 2 inches. Cover and let stand at room temperature overnight. (Or, in a 6-qt sauce pot, place beans and enough water to cover by 2 inches. Heat to boiling over high heat; cook 2 minutes.

Remove from heat; cover and let stand 1 hour.) Drain and rinse beans.

-In 4 1/2 to 5 1/2 quart Crockpot, stir 3 1/2 cups water with beans and remaining ingredients except salt until blended.

-Cover CP with lid and cook beans on low setting about 14 hours or until beans are tender and sauce is syrupy. Stir salt into bean mixture before serving.

CROCKPOT BOURBON BREAST OF CHICKEN
4 chicken breasts halves
1/4 c flour
1/2 tsp paprika
Salt
2 tbsp butter
2 tbsp oil
2 tbsp onion, chopped
2 tbsp parsley, chopped
1/4 tsp dried chervil
1/4 c bourbon
1 (4 oz) can mushrooms, undrained
1 (10 oz) can tomatoes
1/4 tsp sugar
Salt & Pepper

Dredge chicken in flour which has been mixed with paprika and a little salt. Heat butter and oil in a skillet and saute chicken on both sides until lightly browned. Stir in onion, parsley and chervil and cook a moment. Remove from heat. Place chicken in crock cooker. Combine remaining ingredients and pour over chicken. Cover and cook on LOW for 6 to 7 hours. Serve with noodles of rice. Serves 4

CROCKPOT BRACIOLE
2 1/2 pounds Round steak
1/4 to 1/2" thick 1/2 pound Bulk Italian sausage
1 tablespoon Dried parsley flakes
1/2 teaspoon Leaf oregano

2 cloves Garlic -- minced
1 large Onion -- finely chopped
1 teaspoon Salt
1 can Italian style tomatoes -- 16 0z
1 can tomato paste -- (6 oz)
1 teaspoon Salt
1 teaspoon Leaf oregano
10 large Tomatoes or 2 28 oz cans tomatoes
5 cloves Garlic -- chopped
1 tablespoon Worcestershire sauce
2 teaspoons Salt
2 large Onions -- chopped
1 tablespoon Flour
1 tablespoon Vegetable oil
1 teaspoon Oregano
1 teaspoon Thyme
1 tablespoon Wine vinegar
1 tablespoon Sugar

-Trim all excess fat from round steak. Cut into 8 evenly shaped pieces. Pound steak pieces between waxed paper until very thin and easy to roll. In skillet, lightly brown sausage. Drain well and combine with parsley, 1/2 teaspoon oregano, garlic, onion, and salt; mix well. Spread each steak with 2 to 3 tablespoons of sausage mixture. Roll up steaks and tie. Stack steak rolls in crock pot. Combine tomatoes, tomato paste, salt, and 1 teaspoon oreagno; pour over rolls. Cover and cook on low setting for 8 to 10 hours. Serve steak rolls with sauce.

-SAUCE: Place all ingredients except flour, oil, and vinegar in crockpot; stir well. Cover and cook on low setting for 8 to 10 hours. Remove cover and turn to high setting for the last hour to reduce excess moisture. Before removing sauce from crock pot, stir in flour, oil, and vinegar. Allow to cool. Pour 3 cups of sauce at a time into blender container; blend until smooth.

CROCKPOT BRAISED CHICKEN CURRY WITH YAMS
Canola oil
2 lbs chicken legs and thighs (I use bonless/skinless thighs mostly)
2 large white onions chopped

1 tbsp minced garlic
1 tbsp minced ginger
1/3 cup madras curry powder (mild, medium/hot your choice)
1 banana
2 bay leaves
4 cups chicken stock
3 large yams, peeled and chopped
salt and black pepper to taste

In a hot stock pot coated with oil, season the chicken and brown on all sides. Put chicken aside. IN the same stockpot, remove all chicken fat, leaving only a coating of oil and saute onions, garlic and ginger. Caramelize well, then add curry powder. Mix quickly for 2 minutes making sure not to burn the curry powder. Add back the chicken, banana, bay leaves,yams and chicken stock. Check for seasonings. Briing to a boil and then simmer slowly for 1 1/2 - 2 hours.

Serve on basmati rice. I usually toss it all into the crockpot when i add back the chicken etc.... and leave it on low for about 4 hours.

CROCKPOT BREAKFAST CASSEROLE
4 medium-sized apples, peeled and sliced
1/4 cup honey
1 tsp. cinnamon
2 Tbs. butter, melted
2 cups granola cereal

Place apples in slow cooker and mix in remaining ingredients. Cover and cook on LOW for 7-9 hours (overnight). Serve with milk.

CROCKPOT BROCCOLI SOUP
4 c. water
4 chicken bouillon cubes
1/4 c. chopped onion
2 c. diced potatoes
1 bag frozen, chopped broccoli
2 cans cream of chicken soup
1/2-1 lb. Velveeta cheese, cubed

Mix water, bouillon cubes, onions, potatoes and broccoli in a crock pot. Cook on high until broccoli is thawed. Add cream of chicken soup and cheese, to taste, to mixture. Turn crock pot on low and cook for 2 hours.

CROCKPOT BROCCOLI SOUP WITH A LITTLE HELP
Serving Size : 8
4 tablespoons margarine
1/2 cup finely chopped celery
1 cup chopped onion
1 carrots -- thinly sliced (1 to 2)
1 cup water
1/4 cup rice
1/8 teaspoon cayenne pepper
2 heads broccoli (about a pound)
1 can cream of broccoli soup
3 cups 2% low-fat milk
paprika -- for garnish

Saute onion, carrot slices and celery in margarine until tender. Stir in water, rice, pepper, and cream of broccoli soup. Stir until smooth. Cover and cook over low to medium heat for 15 minutes. Cut off broccoli stems and slice into very thin pieces - the size of a match stick. Separate tops into florets and steam broccoli until tender. Save a few tops for garnish. Stir broccoli into soup and cook until everything is tender and hot. Now you have a choice. You can place a whole batch of soup into your blender, add the milk and blend until smooth. Or, you can put just half the soup in your blender - add the milk and still have some whole pieces of veggies to eat or you can just add the milk and leave all the pieces of veggies alone and enjoy the soup like it is. Anyway, you want to reheat the soup but do not boil. Garnish bowls of soup with paprika and broccoli florets. NOTES : you can leave the cream of broccoli soup out, if you wish, but it does add a little more body and a few more interesting tastes to the dish.

CROCKPOT BROWN RICE AND CHICKEN
1 c. diced cooked chicken
2 onions, chopped
2 stalks celery, chopped
2 c. cooked brown rice
1/4 c. dry white wine
2 c. chicken broth

1 c. sliced almonds

Combine all ingredients in slow cooker. Cook on low 6 to 8 hours or on automatic 4 to 5 hours. Serve with sliced almonds lightly toasted.

CROCKPOT BRUNCH CASSEROLE

Serving Size : 7
1 1/2 lb Ground beef
1 ea Onion -- large; finely chopped
2 tb Olive oil or butter
2 ea Garlic -- cloves; minced
1 cn Mushrooms -- sliced; drained; 4 oz
2 ts Salt
1/2 ts Nutmeg
1/2 ts Oregano -- leaf
1/2 pk Spinach -- chopped; frozen*
3 tb Flour
6 ea Eggs -- beaten
1/4 c Milk -- scalded
1/2 c Cheddar cheese -- sharp; grated
*thawed;drained

In skillet, lightly brown ground beef and onion in olive oil; drain well. (I like

to saute fresh mushrooms instead of using canned.) Place in well-greased crock-pot.

Stir in remaining ingredients except eggs, milk and cheese until well blended. Beat eggs and milk together. Pour over other ingredients; stir well. Dust with additional nutmeg. Cover and cook on LOW setting for 7 to 10 hours or until firm.

Just before serving, sprinkle with grated cheese. 6 to 8 servings (About 2-1/2 quarts)

Yummy! I recommend the 10 hours on low though, any less and the eggs are runny...

CROCKPOT CABBAGE AND BEEF CASSEROLE

2 lb. ground beef
1 head cabbage, shredded
1 small onion, chopped

1 (16oz) can tomatoes
broth or tomato juice to cover bottom of pot
Garlic salt, thyme, red pepper and a bit of oregano
Brown ground beef and drain. Shred cabbage and chop onion.
Put in broth or other liquid to cover bottom of pot. Layer cabbage,
onion, spices, meat, and garlic salt.

Repeat layers ending with beef. Top with tomatoes, undrained
and a dusting of oregano. Cook on high for 1 hour. Stir all together.
Cook on low heat until ready to eat, 8-10 hours. Makes 3-4 servings.

CROCKPOT CABBAGE BURGER BAKE
6 cups shredded cabbage and carrots
3/4 pound lean ground beef
1/2 teaspoon salt
1/4 teaspoon ground black pepper
1 medium onion -- finely chopped
1 cup long-grain rice
1 26 oz. can chunky low-fat spaghetti sauce
1/2 cup water
1/4 teaspoon dried basil leaves -- crushed
1/4 teaspoon seasoned salt

Place 1/2 of the cabbage and carrots in a slow cooker. Crumble ground beef over top. Sprinkle 1/4 teaspoon of the salt and 1/8 teaspoon of the pepper. Evenly distribute onion, then rice over all. Top with remaining cabbage, salt, and pepper. Combine spaghetti sauce, water, basil, and seasoned salt; pour over cabbage. Cover and cook on LOW 5 to 6 hours or until rice is tender.

CROCKPOT CABBAGE CHILI SOUP
3 cups coarsely chopped cabbage
1 cup chopped onions
3 cups Healthy Choice tomato juice (or any reduced-sodium)
1 (10-1/2 oz) can Healthy Request Tomato Soup
10 oz kidney beans, rinsed and drained
2 tsp chili seasoning mix In a slow cooker, combine cabbage, onion, tomato juice and tomato soup. Add kidney beans and chili

seasoning mix. Mix well to combine. Cover and cook on LOW for 6-8 hours. Mix well before serving.

Great recipe for diabetics, dieters.

CROCKPOT CAFE CHICKEN

4 lbs cut up chicken
1 onion chopped
2 (or more) cloves of garlic, chopped (not pressed)
1 green pepper chopped
1 medium ripe tomato, peeled & chopped (I omitted, didn't have)
1 cup dry white wine
Pinch of Cayenne pepper

Combine all ingredients in slow-cooker. Cover, set on low and cook for 6-8 hours. If you want you can cook for 5 1/2 and then place chicken on cookie sheets with sides (jelly roll pan)and cook for 30-45 minutes at 350°F to crisp up skin. Serve with crusty french bread. Serves 4-5.

CROCKPOT CAJUN SAUSAGE & RICE

8oz Kielbasa sausage, cut in 1/4" slices
1 (14 1/2oz) can diced Tomatoes with liquid
1 medium Onion, diced
1 medium Green Pepper, diced
2 Celery stalks, thinly sliced
1 TBSP Chicken bouillon granules
1 TBSP Steak sauce
3 Bay leaves or 1 tsp dried Thyme
1 TSP sugar
1/4 to 1/2 TSP Hot Pepper sauce
1 cup uncooked instant Rice
1/2 cup chopped Parsley (optional)

Combine sausage, tomatoes, onion, green pepper, celery bouillon, steak sauce, bay leaves, sugar and hot pepper sauce in crockpot. Cover and cook on LOW for 8 hours.

Remove bay leaves; stir in rice and 1/2 cup of water. Cook an additional 25 minutes. Stir in parsley if desired.

Makes 5 servings

CROCKPOT CANTONESE DINNER
1 1/2 lb pork steak 1/2" thick cut into strips
2 Tbsp oil
1 onion large, sliced
1 green pepper small cut into strips
1 4 oz mushroom, drained
1 8 oz tomato sauce can
3 Tbsp brown sugar
1 1/2 Tbsp vinegar
1 1/2 tsp salt
2 tsp worcestershire sauce
Directions:
Brown pork in oil in skillet. Drain on double paper towel. Place pork strips and all remaining ingr. into crock pot. Cover and cook on low for 6 to 8 Hr (high 4 hr) Serve over hot fluffy rice.

CROCKPOT CANTONESE PORK DINNER
2 pounds pork steaks
2 tablespoons vegetable oil
1 onion, thinly sliced
1 (4.5 ounce) can mushrooms, drained
1 (8 ounce) can tomato sauce
3 tablespoons brown sugar
1 1/2 teaspoons distilled white vinegar
1 1/2 teaspoons salt
2 tablespoons Worcestershire sauce
In a heavy skillet, heat oil over medium high heat. Add pork strips and brown.

Drain off excess fat. Place meat, onion, mushrooms, tomato sauce, brown sugar, vinegar, salt, and Worcestershire sauce in a slow cooker. Cook on High for 4 hours, or on Low for 6 to 8 hours. Serve hot.

CROCKPOT CAPONATA

1 lb plum tomatoes chopped
1 eggplant in 1/2" pieces
2 med zucchini in 1/2" pieces
1 onion finely chopped
3 stalks celery sliced
1/2 c chopped parsley
2 Tbsp red wine vinegar
1 Tbsp brown sugar
1/4 c raisins
1/4 c tomato paste
1 tsp salt
1/4 tsp freshly ground black pepper
3 Tbsp oil cured black olives (optional)
2 Tbsp capers (optional)

Combine tomatoes, eggplant, zucchini, celery, onion, parsley, vinegar, sugar, raisins, tomato paste, salt & pepper in crock pot. Cook, covered on low heat for 5 1/2 hours. Do not remove cover during cooking. Stir in olives & capers, if using.

Serve warm or cold.

CROCKPOT CARAMEL APPLE EUPHORIA DESSERT

2 md Cooking apples
1/2 c Apple juice
7 oz Caramel candy squares
1 ts Vanilla
1/8 ts Ground cardamom
1/2 ts Ground cinnamon
1/3 c Cream-style peanut butter
7 sl Angel-food cake; or
1 qt Vanilla ice cream

Peel, core, and cut each apple into 18 wedges; set aside. Combine apple juice, unwrapped caramel candies, vanilla, cardamom and cinnamon. Drop peanut butter 1 teaspoon at a time, over ingredients in crockpot. Stir. Add apple wedges; cover and cook on LOW for 5 hours. Stir thoroughly; cover and cook on LOW 1 additional hour.

Serve approximately 1/3 cup of warm mixture over a slice of angel food cake or ice cream.

Serves 7.

CROCKPOT CARAMEL APPLES
2 packages (14oz) bags caramels
1/4 cup Water
8 Medium apples

In crockpot, combine caramels and water. Cover and cook on high for 1 to 1 ½ hours, stirring frequently. Wash and dry apples. Insert stick into stem end of each apple. Turn control on low. Dip apple into hot caramel and turn to coat entire surface. Holding apple above pot, scrape off excess accumulation of caramel from bottom apple. Place on greased wax paper to cool.

CROCKPOT CARAMEL PIE
Serving Size : 8
2 Packages (14 oz) bags caramels
1/4 Cup water
8 Medium apples

In crockpot, combine caramels and water. Cover and cook on high for 1 to 1 ½ hours, stirring frequently. Wash and dry apples. Insert stick into stem end of each apple. Turn control on low. Dip apple into hot caramel and turn to coat entire surface. Holding apple above pot, scrape off excess accumulation of caramel from bottom apple. Place on greased wax paper to cool.

CROCKPOT CARAMEL RUM FONDUE
Serving Size : 12
7 ounces caramels
1/4 cup miniature marshmallows
1/3 cup whipping cream
2 teaspoons rum or 1/4 t rum extract

Combine caramels and cream in crock pot. Cover and heat until melted, 30 to 60 minutes. Stir in marshmallows and rum. Cover and continue cooking 30 minutes. Serve with apple wedges or pound cake.

CROCKPOT CARNE GISADA

3 lbs beef stew meat
2 cans diced ROTEL tomatoes with green chilis
salt and peper to taste
3 cloves garlic minced
1 cup chopped onion
3 TBSP flour
1/2 tsp cumin
1/2 tsp oregeno
1 tsp chili powder
1/4 cup water
1 diced bell pepper

Place stew meat, 1/4 cup water, salt and pepper in crockpot. turn heat to high and let simmer for 1 1/2 hours. Drain juice from tomatoes into measuring cup. Add tomoatoes garlic and onions to crock pot STIR let simmer on high for 30 minutes. Add cumin, oregeno, and chili powder to crock pot and stir. Blend juice and enough water to equal 1 1/2 cups liquid and flour stir into meat/veggie mixture. Let cook on LOW for 3-4 hours until sauce is nice and thick (if you like runnier gravy three

hours is good) Serve with warm flour tortillas.

CROCKPOT CARROT CHICKEN

skinless, boneless chicken breasts
1 medium head cabbage, quartered
1 pound carrots, cut into 1" pieces
water to cover
4 cubes chicken bouillon
1 teaspoon poultry seasoning
1/4 teaspoon Greek-style seasoning
2 tablespoons cornstarch
1/4 cup water

-Rinse chicken and place in slow cooker. Rinse cabbage and place on top of chicken, then add carrots. Add enough water to almost cover all. Add bouillon cubes and sprinkle liberally with poultry seasoning. Add Greek seasoning to taste (as you would salt and pepper). Cook on low for 8 hours OR on high for 4 hours.

-To Make Gravy: When you're nearly ready to eat, pour off some of the juice and place in a saucepan. Bring to a boil. Dissolve cornstarch in about 1/4 cup water (depending on how thick you like your gravy). Add to saucepan and simmer all together until thick. If desired, season with additional Greek seasoning.

Serve gravy over chicken and potatoes, if desired.

CROCKPOT CATALINA RIBS
1 1/2-2 lbs boneless pork ribs
1 onion chopped
2 cloves garlic, minced
1 (8 oz) bottle of Catalina

Place or throw ribs in crock pot. Put in rest of ingredients and cook low for 5-7 hours.

CROCKPOT CHEESE AND MEATBALL SOUP
Serving Size : 6
2 cups water
1 cup corn -- whole kernel
1 cup potato -- chopped
1 cup celery -- chopped
1/2 cup carrot -- sliced
1/2 cup onion -- chopped
2 cubes beef bouillon
1 jar cheez whiz -- (16 oz) meatballs
1 pound ground beef
1/4 cup bread crumbs
1 large egg
1/2 teaspoon salt
1/2 teaspoon tabasco sauce
Meatballs:

Mix ingredients together thoroughly. Shape into medium size meatballs. Place uncooked meatballs and all other ingredients, except Cheez Whiz, in electric slow cooker. Stir gently. Cover and cook on setting # 2 (low) for 8 to 10 hours. Before serving add Cheez Whiz, stirring gently until well blended.

NOTES : Serve with a crusty bread.

CROCKPOT CHEESE DIP
* 2 lb. Velveeta cheese
* 2 cans Rotel tomatoes and chilies
* 1 can cream of mushroom soup
* 1 sm. jar picante sauce
* 1 tsp. garlic powder
* Dash of Worcestershire
* 1 lb. premium ground beef
* 1 med. onion, chopped
* 1 lb. sausage

Mix all of the liquids and cheese together in a Crock Pot set on low until the cheese melts. While this is cooking, brown meats and chopped onion. Drain grease off of meats and add spices, then add to Crock Pot and stir. Cook on low 2 to 4 hours, keep on low to serve with chips and crackers.

CROCKPOT CHEESE FONDUE
* 10-oz. can cheddar cheese soup
* 1 lb block process cheese spread cut in 8 pieces
* 1 lb swiss cheese, grated
* 12-oz. can beer (or apple cider)
* 1/2 tsp hot pepper sauce
* 2 drops liquid smoke flavoring

Place all ingredients in slow cooker/Crock Pot. Stir to mix. Cover and cook on low for 2 hours. After 1 hour of cooking time, stir. Before serving, whisk to blend.

Serve with bread sticks or veggies for dipping.

CROCKPOT CHEESE SOUFFLE
14 slices fresh white bread, crust removed
3 c. grated sharp cheese, Cheddar
1/4 c. oleo
6 lg. eggs
3 c. milk, scalded
2 tbsp. Worcestershire sauce

1/2 tsp. salt

Paprika

Tear bread in small pieces. Place 1/2 in well greased crock pot. Add 1/2 cheese, 1/2 butter. Add remaining bread, cheese and butter. Beat eggs, milk, Worcestershire sauce and salt. Pour over bread and cheese. Sprinkle with paprika. Cover and cook on low 4-6 hours. Do not open until ready to serve.

CROCKPOT CHEESE SOUP

1/2 stick butter
3 green onions -- chopped
3 stalks celery with leaves -- chopped
2 carrots -- grated
2 cans chicken broth
2 cans cheese soup
1 can cream of potato soup
parsley flakes
tabasco sauce -- to taste
salt and pepper -- to taste
8 ounces sour cream/or plain nonfat yogurt
3 tablespoons cooking sherry

Melt butter over low heat and saute onions, celery and carrots. Add chicken broth; cover and simmer for 30 minutes. Add other soups, parsley, tabasco, salt & pepper. Stir in sour cream. Simmer 15 minutes. Add sherry and stir before serving.

CROCKPOT CHEESY BACON DIP

2 pkgs (8 oz) cream cheese, softened, cut into cubes
4 cups shredded Colby-Jack Cheese
1 cup half-and-half
2 T mustard
1 T chopped onion
2 tsp Worcestershire sauce
1/2 tsp salt
1/4 tsp hot pepper sauce

1 lb bacon, cooked and crumbled

Place cream cheese, Colby-Jack cheese, half-and-half, mustard, onion,

Worcestershire sauce, salt and pepper sauce in crock pot. Cover and cook, stirring occasionally, on low 1 hour or until cheese melts. Stir in bacon; adjust seasonings.

Serve with crusty bread or crackers.

CROCKPOT CHEESY CHICKEN ALA TIFFANY

1 can mushroom soup

1 can cream of broccoli soup

1 can broccoli cheese soup

2 pkgs Chicken Breasts (boneless, skinless)

1 can Mixed vegetables

1-2 T Tapioca for thickening

1 cup shredded cheddar cheese

Dice chicken put in crockpot sprinkle with salt and pepper, Pour all three cans of soup over chicken and stir. Cover and cook on low about 4-6 hours. About an hour before serving add mixed vegies, cheese and thicken with tapioca. I served poured over white rice. I thought the flavors blended and complemented each other well.

CROCKPOT CHEESY CREAMED CORN

3 16 oz. pkgs frozen corn

1 8 oz. pkg cream cheese

1 3 oz. pkg cream cheese

4 TBLSP butter

3 TBLSP water

3 TBLSP milk

2 TBLSP sugar

6 slices American cheese

Combine all ingredients in cp, mix well. Cover and cook 4 - 5 hours on low, or until heated through and cheese is melted. Stir well before serving.

CROCKPOT CHICKEN I

1 frying chicken, cut up
Salt & pepper
1 can cream of mushroom soup
1/2 c. sauterne or sherry
2 tbsp. butter or margarine, melted
2 tbsp. dry Italian salad dressing mix
2 (3 oz.) pkgs. cream cheese, cut in cubes
1 tbsp. onion, chopped
Wash chicken and pat dry. Brush with butter. Sprinkle with salt and pepper. Place in crock pot. Sprinkle with dry salad mix. Cover and cook on low for 5 to 6 hours.

About 3/4 hour before serving, mix soup, cream cheese, wine, and onion in small saucepan. Cook until smooth. Pour over chicken in pot. Cover and cook for 30 minutes on low. Serve with sauce. Serve with rice or noodles.

Serves 4 to 6.

CROCKPOT CHICKEN II
1 large chicken, cut-up
2 c. soy sauce
2 c. vinegar
Put in crockpot and cook on high 4-5 hours.

CROCKPOT CHICKEN ALA KING
1 can cream of chicken soup
3 tbsp. flour
1/4 tsp. pepper
Dash of cayenne pepper
1 lb. boneless, skinless chicken breasts, cut into cubes
I celery rib, chopped
1/2 c. chopped green pepper
1/4 c. chopped onion
1 package (10 oz.) frozen peas, thawed
2 tbsp. diced pimentos, drained
Hot cooked rice
Combine soup, flour and peppers in crock pot, stir until smooth. Stir in chicken, celery, onion and green pepper. Cover and

cook on low 7-8 hours or until meat is cooked through. Stir in peas and pimentos. Cook 30 minutes longer. Serve over rice.

CROCKPOT CHICKEN AND DUMPLINGS
4 Tablespoons butter
1 Tablespoon vegetable oil
1 onion -- chopped
3 pounds your favorite chicken parts -- cut up
2 cups chicken broth
2 stalks celery
1 tablespoon minced parsley
2 carrots -- peeled, sliced
1 tsp black pepper
Salt to taste
1/2 tsp ground allspice
1 cup dry white wine (optional but really adds a nice taste)
1 can refrigerated biscuits
1/2 cup heavy cream
2 tablespoons flour

In a large skillet, brown onion in butter and oil just until tender, then brown chicken parts and place all in a 6-quart crockpot. Add remaining ingredients except heavy cream, flour and biscuits. Cook on high 2-1/2 to 3 hours, or on low 5 to 7 hours. When chicken is done, remove pieces to plate and let cool, then debone.

While chicken is cooling, mix flour and cream together, then stir into crockpot. Open biscuits and cut each biscuit into 4 pieces. Drop into crockpot and turn on high. These will need to cook about 30 minutes, until they are firm. Return chicken meat to crockpot after deboning and serve. You can use your own homemade biscuit recipe for canned if you prefer.

CROCKPOT CHICKEN & NOODLES
4 carrots, sliced
4-5 pieces chicken
1 small onion, chopped
2 cups water
4 chicken bouillon cubes

1 tsp garlic salt
salt & pepper, to taste
1 lb egg noodles
Place carrots in CP, followed by all ingredients except noodles. Cook on LOW for 8 hours. At the end of cooking time, cook egg noodles on stovetop. While noodles cook, remove chicken from CP & cut into bite-size pieces. Return chicken & noodles to CP. If desired, thicken broth with cornstarch & water. Just be sure to add some of the broth to your cornstarch mixture first. This will prevent any lumps from forming.

CROCKPOT CHICKEN AND PASTA

1 T cooking oil
1 lb boneless skinless chicken breasts (cut into bite sized pieces)
1 can of Cream of Chicken soup
1/2 cup water
1 bag frozen seasoned pasta and veggie combo (I like the one with corkscrew pasta and cheddar cheese)
Heat the oil and then brown the chicken in it. Set the chicken aside and add soup, water, and the pasta/veggie combo. Heat to a boil. Return the chicken to the pan and reduce the heat to low. Cover and cook for 5 min. or until the chicken is no longer pink. Stir occasionally. Serves about 4.

CROCKPOT CHICKEN AND RICE I

Boneless, skinless chicken breast (2-3 lbs)
Chicken Flavored Rice (I use Lipton)
Cream of Celery soup
Cream of Chicken soup
1 cup water
salt
Put rice in crockpot, and water. Combine soups and layer on top of rice. Salt chicken and layer chicken in pot. Set on high for 4-5 hours or low or auto shift for 7-10 hours.

CROCKPOT CHICKEN AND RICE II

3/4 c. rice

1 can cream of celery soup
1 can cream of mushroom soup
1 sm. can whole mushrooms
1 sm. jar pimento strips, drained
1/2 green pepper, chopped
1/2 onion, chopped
1 can water chestnuts, drained, sliced
8 to 12 chicken breasts, halved
Grated Parmesan cheese

Place rice in crock pot. Combine remaining ingredients except chicken and cheese in bowl. Mix well. Pour half of mixture over rice. Place chicken on top. Pour remaining soup mixture over all. Cook on high for 3 hours or until chicken is tender. Garnish with cheese.

CROCKPOT CHICKEN AND SAUSAGE PAELLA

2 1/2 to 3 lbs. meaty chicken pieces
1 tbsp. cooking oil
8 oz. cooked smoked turkey sausage, halved lengthwise and sliced
1 large onion, sliced
3 cloves garlic, minced
2 tbsp. snipped fresh thyme or 2 tsp. dried thyme, crushed
1/4 tsp. black pepper
1/8 tsp. thread saffron or 1/4 tsp. ground turmeric
1 141/2 oz. can reduced-sodium chicken broth
1/2 c. water
2 c. chopped tomatoes
2 yellow or green sweet peppers, cut into very thin bite-size strips
1 c. frozen green peas
3 c. hot cooked rice

-Skin chicken. Rinse chicken; pat dry. In a large skillet brown chicken pieces, half at a time, in hot oil. Drain off fat. In a 3 1/2, 4, or 5 quart crockery cooker place chicken pieces, turkey sausage, and onion. Sprinkle with garlic, dried thyme (if using), black pepper, and saffron or turmeric. Pour broth and water over all.

-Cover; cook on low-heat setting for 7 to 8 hours or on high-heat setting for 3 ½ to 4 hours. Add the tomatoes, sweet peppers, peas, and if using, the fresh thyme to the cooker. Cover; let stand for 5 minutes. Serve over the hot rice. Makes 6 servings* Prep time: 30 min.

CROCKPOT CHICKEN CACCIATORE I
1 large onion, thinly sliced
1 1/2 lb. skinless, boneless chicken breasts
2 (6 oz each) cans tomato paste
8 oz. fresh sliced mushrooms
1/2 tsp. salt
1/4 tsp. pepper
2 cloves garlic, minced
1 tsp. oregano
1/2 tsp. basil
1 bay leaf
1/4 c. dry white wine
1/4 c. water

Put sliced onion in bottom of crock pot. Add chicken pieces. Stir together tomato paste, mushrooms, salt, pepper, garlic, herbs, white wine and water. Spread over chicken. Cover; cook on Low 7 to 9 hours (High: 3 to 4 hours). Serve chicken pieces over hot spaghetti or vermicelli. 4 servings.

CROCKPOT CHICKEN CACCIATORE II
1 chicken (5 pounds), cut into pieces
1/4 cup olive oil
1 cup flour
1 cup chopped onions
1 cup sliced mushrooms
1 cup julienned carrot
1 cup julienned green pepper
2 Tablespoons minced garlic
8 cups chopped, peeled tomatoes
1/2 cup tomato paste
3/4 cup red or Marsala wine
1 teaspoon oregano
1 teaspoon basil
1 1/2 teaspoons salt

1 teaspoon pepper
freshly grated Romano cheese

Wash and drain the chicken pieces. Heat the oil in a deep skillet. Roll and coat each chicken piece in the flour and brown each piece on all sides to a golden brown. Transfer the chicken to paper towels to drain. Saute the onion, mushrooms, carrots, green peppers, and garlic in the same skillet for 10 minutes. Add the tomatoes and saute for another 5 minutes. Stir in the tomato paste, wine, herbs, salt and pepper, and cook over medium heat for another 5 minutes.

Add all the chicken pieces and mix well. Turn down the heat very low, and simmer, covered, for 1 hour. Adjust the salt and pepper to your taste. Serve with some freshly grated cheese and a nice warm loaf of Italian bread. I made this up just like it says and then took it all and threw it in the crock. Its been there since 1pm and we will probably eat between 5 and 6pm. For me the longer a sauce simmers the better it tastes. You can also serve it over linguini noodles! YUMMMMMMMM

CROCKPOT CHICKEN CACCIATORE III

1 can tomatoes, diced (a small can probably, I actually had to open a 6# can and
just put a few scoops in)
2 cans (small ones) tomato paste
1/2 c. dry white wine
1 can mushrooms (usually I use fresh, but these were on hand, so I used 'em! lol)
1 small onion, sliced
4 cloves garlic, sliced
1 Tbl Italian Seasoning
1 tsp basil
1 tsp oregano

I mixed all those together and poured it over the top of the chicken. Then I cooked it on LOW all day (started it around 9 I think, cooked til 6)

CROCKPOT CHICKEN CASSEROLE

4 lg. chicken breasts

1 sm. can cream of chicken soup
1 sm. can cream of celery soup
1 sm. can cream of mushroom soup
1/2 c. diced celery
1 c. Minute Rice

Mix in crockpot the soups and rice. Place chicken on top of mixture, then sprinkle diced celery over chicken. Cook on low for 4 hours. Makes 4 servings.

CROCKPOT CHICKEN CORDON BLEU

4-6 chicken breasts (pounded out thin)
4-6 pieces of ham
4-6 slices of swiss cheese (I use mozzerella,my kids like this better!)
1 can cream of mushroom soup(can use any cream soup)
1/4 c. milk

Put ham and cheese on chicken. Roll up and secure with a toothpick. Place chicken in c.p. so it looks like a triangle /_\ Layer the rest on top. Mix soup and milk. Pour over top of chicken. Cover and cook on low for 4 hours or until chicken is no longer pink. Serve over noodles with the sauce it makes.

CROCKPOT CHICKEN AND DUMPLINGS

4 Tablespoons butter
1 Tablespoon vegetable oil
1 onion -- chopped
3 pounds your favorite chicken parts -- cut up
2 cups chicken broth
2 stalks celery
1 tablespoon minced parsley
2 carrots -- peeled, sliced
1 tsp black pepper
Salt to taste
1/2 tsp ground allspice
1 cup dry white wine (optional but really adds a nice taste)
1 can refrigerated biscuits
1/2 cup heavy cream

2 tablespoons flour

In a large skillet, brown onion in butter and oil just until tender, then brown
chicken parts and place all in a 6-quart crockpot.

Add remaining ingredients except heavy cream, flour and biscuits. Cook on high 2- 1/2 to 3 hours, or on low 5 to 7 hours.

When chicken is done, remove pieces to plate and let cool, then debone. While chicken is cooling, mix flour and cream together, then stir into crockpot. Open biscuits and cut each biscuit into 4 pieces. Drop into crockpot and turn on high.

These will need to cook about 30 minutes, until they are firm. Return chicken meat to crockpot after deboning and serve. You can use your own homemade biscuit recipe for canned if you prefer.

CROCKPOT CHICKEN ENCHILADAS I

boneless, skinless chicken (can still be frozen)
1 large can enchilada sauce (green or red)
medium or large flour tortillas
shredded cheese

Empty enchilada sauce into the crockpot and place chicken filets into the sauce.

Cook on low setting all day. Scoop out chicken and cut or shred onto a plate.

Spread a tortilla on another plate and arrange some chicken into a "stripe" down the middle. Sprinkle liberal shredded cheese, and ladle some sauce over it. Roll the tortilla up, ladle more sauce over it, and sprinkle more cheese. Place in the microwave for about 20 seconds on High to melt the cheese. More microwave time may be needed for multiple enchiladas on one plate.

CROCKPOT CHICKEN ENCHILADAS II

1 Lg. can Enchilada sauce
4 chicken breasts
2 cans cream of chicken soup
1 sm. can sliced black olives
2 dozen corn tortillas
1 chopped onion
1 pkg sharp cheddar cheese

Cook chicken and shred. Mix soup, olives and onions. Cut tortillas in wedges. Layer crockpot with sauce, tortillas, soup mix, chicken and cheese all the way to top, ending with cheese on top. Cook on low temp all day.

CROCKPOT CHICKEN FRICASSEE
Reduced Fat
1 can reduced fat cream of chicken soup
1/2 soup can water
1/2 cup chopped onions
1 teaspoon paprika
1 teaspoon lemon juice
1 teaspoon rosemary
1 teaspoon thyme
1 teaspoon salt
1/4 teaspoon pepper
4 skinless boneless chicken breast
non-stick cooking spray

Spray crockpot with non-stick cooking spray. Place chicken in crockpot. Mix remaining ingredients together and pour over chicken. Cover and cook on low 6-8 hours.

1 hour before serving, prepare chive dumplings:
3 tbl. shortening
1 1/2 cups flour
2 tsp. baking powder
3/4 tsp. salt
3 tbl.fresh, chopped chives, or 2 tbl. dried chives
3/4 cup skim milk

Mix dry ingredients and shortening. Add chives and milk, combine well. Drop by teaspoonsful onto hot chicken and gravy. Cover and cook on high for 45-60 minutes.

Serve with mashed potatoes and vegetables, or over hot, cooked noodles.

CROCKPOT CHICKEN FRIED CHOPS
(Quick Cooking)
1/2 cups all purpose flour
2 tsp salt

1 1/2 tsp ground mustard
1/2 tsp garlic powder
6 pork chops, trimmed
2 Tbsp vegetable oil
1 can condensed cream of chicken soup, undiluted
1/3 cup water
In a shallow bowl, combine flour, salt, mustard and garlic powder; dredge pork chops. In a skillet, brown the chops on both sides in oil. Place in a slow cooker or crockpot. Combine soup and water; pour over chops. Cover and cook on low for 6-8 hours or until meat is tender. If desired, thicken pan juices and serve with the pork chops.

CROCKPOT CHICKEN IN A POT
3 lb whole chicken
2 carrots, sliced
2 onions, sliced
2 celery stalks with leaves,
1 ts basil
2 ts salt
1/2 ts black pepper
1/2 c chIcken broth or wine
Put carrots, onions, and celery in bottom of CROCK-POT. Add whole chicken. Top with salt, pepper, liquid. Sprinklebasil over top. Cover and cook until done-low 8 to 10 hours. (High 3 to 4 hours, using 1 cup water). Remove chicken and vegetables with spatula. I would suggest thawing chicken before cooking in the crockpot for sure--I don't
think it would be safe to let it go from frozen to cooked over such a long period of time.

CROCKPOT CHICKEN IN SPICY SAUCE
1/2 cup tomato juice
1/2 cup soy sauce
1/2 cup brown sugar
1/4 cup chicken broth
3 cloves garlic minced

1 whole chicken, cut in skinless serving size pieces or favorite parts

Combine all ingredients except chicken in a bowl. Dip each peice of chicken in the sauce. Place in the slow cooker. Pour remaining sauce over the top. Cook on low for 6-8 hours or high 3-4 hours. Makes 6 servings.

CROCKPOT CHICKEN N NOODLES
2 1/2 to 3 1/2 pound broiler/fryer chicken cut up
1 cup chicken broth
2 cups water
1 package (8 ounces) egg noodles
Salt and pepper to taste

Place chicken in crock-pot. Season with salt and pepper; add all liquid. Cover and cook on Low 8 to 10 hours (High 4 to 5 hours) Remove chicken from broth. Turn crockpot to high and add noodles. Bone chicken and cut up meat. Stir chicken into noodles. Cover and cook 30 to 45 minutes, stirring occasionally.

CROCKPOT CHICKEN NOODLE SOUP NEW ORLEANS STYLE
1 lg Whole fryer
1/2 c Diced celery
4 ea Cloves minced garlic
3 ea Bay leaves
4 ea Qts water
2 tb Butter
1 c Sliced mushrooms
1/4 c Cream sherry
Green onions for garnish
1 c Diced onions
1/2 c Minced parsley
1 c Chopped carrots
1 ts Poultry seasoning
12 oz Broad egg noodles
1 c Sliced onion rings
1 c Diced carrots
Salt and pepper to taste

First, take the chicken and wash it thoroughly - that means both inside and out! Remove the giblets, scrub out the internal cavity under cold running water, and scrape away anything that doesn't look edible. (But DO NOT remove the chicken skin or any of the fat! You need the skin to make a rich stock.) Next, take a crock pot and place the chicken and giblets into it. Then drop in the diced onions, the ½ cup of chopped carrots and bay leaves, poultry seasoning and *2* quarts of water. Then, with a spoon, evenly distribute the seasoning mixture around the chicken, turn the crock pot to high, and cook for at least six hours (or better still, OVERNIGHT). Remember, the longer you cook, the richer the base stock and the more tender the chicken. (I cooked it overnight) While the chicken is slow-cooking, it's a good time to prepare your noodles. Go ahead and boil them according to package directions... but DO NOT COOK THEM UNTIL DONE! Keep in mind that you're going to drop them into a soup, so you want them el dente (firm), otherwise they'll turn to pure mush by the time you eat them. Furthermore, you want a small percent of the starch in the noodles to cook into the soup to thicken it slightly - if you cook the noodles all the way, the soup's consistency will be flat and thin. After the noodles are cooked, butter them slightly and set them aside. When the chicken is tender, take a set of tongs or a strainer spoon, remove it from the crock pot (it may tend to fall apart, but that's okay), and set it on a platter to cool. At this point, strain out all the seasoning vegetables from the stock, place the stock into a metal bowl, and place the bowl into the refrigerator or freezer until the chicken fat congeals (which should take about 1 hour). Meanwhile, pick the chicken off the bones and, with a sharp knife, chop it into bite-sized pieces. Then, in a heavy 12- inch skillet, melt the butter and saute the sliced onions, mushrooms, and carrots until they're tender. Then drop in the chopped chicken meat. And over medium-low heat, cook it into the vegetables for about 10 minutes. While the chicken and vegetables are sauteing, remove the chicken stock from the refrigerator, skim off all the fat, and place the skimmed stock into a soup pot, along with the remaining 2 quarts of water. At this point, you should season the soup stock to taste with salt and pepper. Now drop in the sauteed chicken, mushrooms, onion rings and diced carrots - along with the sherry, the Tabasco, and as soon as it comes to a boil, reduce the heat to low and simmer the soup about 30 minutes to allow all the flavors to thoroughly blend. When you're ready to eat, ladle out heaping helpings of the piping hot soup into bowls, garnish with a sprinkling of thinly sliced green onions, and serve with crunch saltines. I used several generous shakes of Tabasco. It was spicy, but not overwhelmingly hot and fiery. And it was HEAVENLY!

CROCKPOT CHICKEN NOODLE SOUP
3 carrots, peeled and cut into chunks
3 stalks celery, cut into chunks
1 large onion, quartered
3 boneless skinless chicken breast halves
2 cans chicken broth-I use the Swansons Healthy Request, fat free
2 to 3 soup cans of water
a generous shake of dried dill and a generous shake of dried parsley
8 oz. noodles - I use the "No Yolks" brand broad noodles
Put vegetables in CP. Add chicken. Pour in broth and water. Add dill and parsley.

Cover and cook on low 8 hours. Remove veggies and chicken from CP. Add noodles, turn to high and heat while you shred the chicken and mince the veggies. I run the veggies through the food processor. Return chicken and veggies to CP and heat through. It takes the noodles about 20 minute to cook. Serves about 6 hungry folks.

I use a 5 qt CP for this. I also use frozen chicken breast right out of the freezer.

CROCKPOT CHICKEN NOODLE SOUP (LOWFAT)
3 carrots, peeled and cut into chunks
3 stalks celery, cut into chunks
1 large onion, quartered
3 boneless skinless chicken breast halves
2 cans chicken broth-I use the Swansons Healthy Request, fat free
2 to 3 soup cans of water
a generous shake of dried dill and a generous shake of dried parsley

8 oz. noodles - I use the "No Yolks" brand broad noodles
Put vegetables in CP. Add chicken. Pour in broth and water. Add dill and parsley. Cover and cook on low 8 hours. Remove veggies and chicken from CP. Add noodles, turn to high and heat while you shred the chicken and mince the veggies. I run the veggies through the food processor. Return chicken and veggies to CP and heat
through. It takes the noodles about 20 minutes to cook.
Serves about 6 hungry folks. I use a 5 qt CP for this. I also use frozen chicken breast right out of the freezer.

CROCKPOT CHICKEN PARMIGIANA
3 Chicken breasts
1 Egg
1 t Salt
1/4 ts Pepper
1 c Dry bread crumbs
1 1/4 c Butter
1 cn Pizza sauce -- 10 1/2 oz
6 slices Mozarella cheese
Parmesan cheese
If using whole chicken breasts, cut in to halves. In bowl beat egg salt and pepper dip chicken into egg. Then coat with crumbs. In large skillet saute chicken in butter. Arrange chicken in pot. Pour pizza sauce over chicken. Cover and cook on low 6 to 8 hours. Add mozzarella cheese, sprinkle parmesan cheese on top. Cover and cook 15 minutes. Makes 6 servings.

I of course altered it a little. I used boneless, skinless breasts and I used six. Instead of plain bread crumbs, I used Italian. I cut the amount of butter in half. For the mozzarella cheese, I used Healthy choice garlic lover's blend. I used fresh grated parmesan and I used a jar of pizza sauce (14 oz).

CROCKPOT CHICKEN PARMIGIANA
3 Chicken breasts
1 Small egg plant sliced
1 Egg
10 1/2 oz Can pizza sauce
1 ts Salt

6 Slices mozzarella cheese
1/4 ts Pepper
1 c Dry bread crumbs
1/2 c Butter

If using whole chicken breasts, cut into halves. In a bowl beat egg, salt, and pepper. Dip chicken into the egg, then coat with crumbs. In a large skillet or crockpot with a browning unit, saute chicken in the butter. Arrange eggplant and the chicken in pot, (place eggplant on the bottom or it will not cook completely.) Pour pizza sauce over the chicken. Cover and cook on low 6 to 8 hours. Add mozzarella cheese; sprinkle Parmesan cheese on top. Cover and cook 15 minutes.

CROCKPOT CHICKEN PIZZA

4 skinless, boneless chicken breast- cut into bite size pieces
1 onion, chopped
1 green bell pepper, chopped
2 large cans tomato sauce
2 large cans diced tomatoes
1 tablespoon dried parsley
1 tablespoon dried oregano
1 tablespoon dried basil
1 tsp. thyme
4 cloves garlic, pressed
1 bay leaf

Place all ingredients in slow cooker. Stir to make sure all chicken is coated well.

Cook on Low setting for 8 hours, until chicken and vegetables are tender.

CROCKPOT CHICKEN/SAUSAGE CASSOULET

1 package Frozen lima beans
1 cup Tomato juice
1 Carrot -- 1/2 inch pcs
1 Stalk celery -- 1/2"pcs
1 Onion -- chopped
1 Clove garlic -- minced
1 Bay leaf
1 teaspoon Chicken bouillon granules

1/2 teaspoon Dried basil -- crushed
1/2 teaspoon Dried oregano -- crushed
3 Boneless chicken breasts
3 Chicken drumsticks
8 ounces Smoked kielbasa

Place carrots, limas, celery and onions on bottom of crockpot which has been sprayed with Pam. Combine herbs, juice and bouillon and add to vegetables. Place chicken on top of vegetables. Cut sausage into pieces. Put chicken and sausage on top of vegs Cover crockpot and cook on Low heat for 10 hours or on high for 5 hours. Remove bay leaf before serving.

CROCKPOT CHICKEN SOUP

2 carrots
2 celery stalks
2 onions
3 boneless, skinless chicken breast
2 tsp salt
1/2 tsp pepper
4 cups chicken broth
4 to 5 cups water
1 T dried parsley
1 T dried dill
6 oz noodles

Slice carrots, celery and onion. Place in crock pot. Add chicken, broth,water, and spices. Cover and cook on low 8 to 10 hours. One hour before serving, remove chicken and vegetables from pot. Add 6oz. noodles to pot, cover and turn to high. While noodles are cooking, shred the chicken and mince the vegetables (I run mine through the food processor). Return chicken and veggies to the pot. Cook til

noodles are done. Use the frozen chicken breasts and put them in frozen-just cook on high for the first hour. Use the chicken broth that is reduced sodium and fat free. Use your favorite noodle type. You can use the "NO Yolks" broad. This can be made in a 3qt pot, but it is a tight fit.

CROCKPOT CHICKEN STEW

Yield: 10 servings

2 lb Chicken breasts/skinless Boneless/ cut in 1" cubes
2 c Fat-free chicken broth
3 c Potatoes; peel, cube
1 c Onion; chop
1 c Celery; sliced
1 c Carrots; sliced thin
1 ts Paprika
1/2 ts Pepper
1/2 ts Rubbed sage
1/2 ts Dried thyme
6 oz No-salt-added tomato paste
1/4 c Cold water
3 tb Cornstarch

In a slow cooker, combine the first 11 ingredients; cover and cook on HIGH for 4 hours. Mix water and cornstarch until smooth; stir into stew. Cook, covered, 30 minutes more or until the vegetables are tender.

CROCKPOT CHICKEN STEW MEXICAN STYLE

2 lbs skinless boneless chicken breasts cut into 1 1/2" peices
4 med russet potatoes, peeled and cut very small
1 (15 oz) can mild salsa
1 (4 oz) can diced green chilies
1 (1 1/4 oz) pkg taco seasoning mix
1 (8oz) can tomato sauce

Mix all ingredients together in crockpot, cook 7-9 hours on low. Serve with warm flour tortillas.

You can also served corn with this. It is good mixed in it too.

CROCKPOT CHICKEN STROGANOFF

1 cup sour cream
1 tablespoon Gold Medal all-purpose flour
1 envelope (.87 to 1.2 oz) chicken gravy mix
1 cup water
1 lb. boneless, skinless chicken breast halves, cut into 1" pieces
1 16 oz. bag frozen stew vegetables, thawed

1 4-oz. jar sliced mushrooms, drained
1 cup frozen peas, thawed
1 1/2 cups Bisquick Original or Reduced Fat baking mix
4 green onions, chopped
1/2 cup milk
Mix sour cream, flour, gravy mix and water in 3 1/2 to 4-quart Crock pot until smooth. Stir in chicken, stew vegetables and mushrooms.

Cover and cook on low heat setting 4 hours or until chicken is tender and sauce is thickened. stir in peas. Mix baking mix and onions. Stir in milk just until moistened. Drop dough by rounded tablespoonfuls onto chicken-vegetable mixture.

Cover and cook on high heat setting 45 to 50 minutes or until toothpick inserted in center of dumplings comes out clean. Serve immediately.

CROCKPOT CHICKEN THIGHS
6 chicken thighs (remove skin)
1 can Italian-style diced tomatoes (28 oz)
salt and pepper
Throw these in the crockpot and cook on high for about 3 hours. Serve with egg noodles. Can it be more simple?!

IF you don't love garlic, use regular tomatoes, but this had a wonderful garlic flavor, we thought. Even the kids liked it, and they usually won't eat anything with sauce. The "sauce" is VERY liquidy, so if you want a more gravy-ish sauce, add some tapioca at the beginning, or partially drain the tomatoes before cooking.

CROCKPOT CHICKEN TORTILLAS
Meat from 1 whole chicken OR canned chicken or parts
1 can cream of chicken soup
1/2 c. green chili salsa
2 tbsp. quick cooking tapioca
1 med. onion, chopped
1 1/2 c. grated cheese
1 doz. corn tortillas
Black olives
Tear chicken into bite size pieces, mix with soup, chili, salsa and tapioca. Line bottom of crock pot with 3 corn tortillas, torn into

bite size pieces. Add 1/3 of the c hicken mixture. Sprinkle with 1/3 of the onion and 1/3 of the grated cheese. Repeat layers of tortillas topped with chicken mixture, onions and cheese. Cover and cook on low 6 to 8 hours or high for 3 hours. Garnish with sliced black olives.

CROCKPOT CHICKEN WINGS
* 5 lb. chicken wings
* 2 c. brown sugar
* 1 c. French's mustard
* 4 tbsp. soy sauce

Cut each wing into 3 pieces - throw away the tip. Brown in skillet until golden brown and put in slow cooker, turn on low heat. Mix brown sugar, mustard and soy sauce in saucepan and heat until it becomes liquid. Pour over the wings and cook 2- 8 hours.

CROCKPOT CHICKEN WITH CHEESE SAUCE
Serves 2

-Place two chicken breast halves in crockpot (frozen or thawed)

-Mix together one can cream of chicken soup & half soup can of white wine; pour over chicken

-Place two slices swiss cheese over top of chicken breasts (processed cheese melts and blends more easily)

-Cook in crockpot for 2-3 hours (on high) or 3-4 hours (on low)

-Serve over steamed rice

(This recipe is also good with a little lemon juice in place of the wine.)

CROCKPOT CHILI I
2 onions, chopped
2 cloves garlic (I use the minced kind that comes in a jar)
1 lb. lean hamburger
2 Tbs. chili powder
cumin to taste (I leave this out)
2 cans (16 oz. ea.) tomatoes
2 cans tomato soup

2 cans kidney beans, drained
salt and pepper to taste
optional: shredded cheese and/or sour cream for topping
1. Cook onions and garlic in 2 Tbs. oil till onions are yellow. Add hamburger and cook till browned. Stir in chili powder and optional cumin; cook 2 minutes more.

Meanwhile, in crockpot, combine remaining ingredients. Stir in browned meat mixture. Cover and cook on Low setting for 8-10 hours.

To serve: ladle chili into bowls. Top with optional shredded cheese and/or sour cream, if desired.

Note: This can be made on top of the stove, too. Let it cook for 1 hour, but stir, so it doesn't stick to the bottom (this is the nice part of using a CP...no need to worry about sticking).

CROCKPOT CHILI II

1 lb ground beef, cooked and rinsed
60-70 ounces rinsed light or dark kidney beans
16 ounces tomato paste
16 ounces peeled chopped tomatoes (reserve liquid)
1/2 small onion, chooped
1 small green pepper, chopped
1 package chili seasonings
cayenne pepper to taste, if desired

Okay, now the hard part, put it all in the crockpot and cook on low until you are ready, I'd recommend at least 5 hours so the peppers and onions are cooked soft. Use the reserved tomato liquid if it seems too thick for your taste. We serve with tortillas, cheese, sour cream, and salsa! Mmmmmmmmmmmm.

CROCKPOT CHILI III

1 16 oz can kidney beans -- drained
2 14 1/2 oz can tomatoes
2 pounds ground chuck -- coarsely ground
2 medium onions -- coarsely chopped
1 green pepper -- coarsely chopped
2 cloves garlic -- crushed
3 tablespoons chili powder

1 teaspoon pepper
1 teaspoon cumin
salt to taste
Put all ingredients in crock pot in order listed. Stir once. Cover and cook on Low 10-12 hours. (High 5-6 hours).
NOTES : Serve with shredded cheddar cheese and tortilla chips.

CROCKPOT CHILI CON CARNE

4 pounds ground beef
3 tablespoons shortening
2 cups chopped onion
2 garlic cloves -- crushed
4 tablespoons chili powder
3 beef bouillon cubes -- crushed
1 1/2 teaspoons paprika
1 teaspoon oregano
1 teaspoon ground cumin
1/2 teaspoon cayenne pepper
1/2 cup beef stock
1 can tomatoes -- 28 ozs.
1 can tomato paste -- 8 oz.
4 cans red kidney beans -- 1 lb cans
Heat shortening in skillet and brown beef, discard fat. Combine all ingredients in removable liner, stirring well. Place liner in base. Cover and cook on low 8-10 hours; high 4-5 hours or auto 6-7 hours.

CROCKPOT CHILI WITH 4 KINDS OF BEANS

1-2 pounds browned ground beef
2 cans chili hot beans
2 cans dark red kidney beans, drained
2 cans pinto beans, drained
2 cans kidney beans, drained
2 cans rotel tomatoes
1 package chili seasoning
Put all ingredients in Crock Pot and cook on low all day (about 10 hours).

CROCKPOT CHINESE PEPPER STEAK

4-6 servings
1-1 1/2 lbs boneless beef round steak
1 clove garlic minced
1/2 tsp. salt
1/4 tsp. pepper
1/4 cup soy sauce
1 Tbls. hoisin sauce
1 tsp. sugar
1 tomato, seeded, peeled & diced
2 red or green bell peppers, cut into strips
3 Tbls. cornstarch
3 Tbls. water
1 cup fresh bean sprouts
4 green onions, finely chopped
Cooked Rice

Trim fat from steak; slice into thin strips. Combine steak, garlic, salt, pepper, soy sauce, hoisin sauce and sugar in slow cooker. Cover and cook on LOW about 4 hours. Turn control to HIGH. Add tomato and bell peppers. Dissolve cornstarch with water in a small bowl and stir into steak mixture. Cover and cook on HIGH 15-20 minutes or until thickened. Stir in bean sprouts, sprinkle with onions. Serve with rice.

CROCKPOT CHINESE PIE

1 to 1 1/2 pounds ground beef
3/4 cup diced bell pepper (green AND red if possible)
3/4 cup diced onion
1 package (dry) brown gravy
4 to 6 medium red or round white potatoes, diced (about 4 cups)
2 tablespoons butter, melted
1 (15 oz) can whole kernel corn, drained (or 2 cups frozen)
1 (15 oz) can creamed corn
salt and pepper to taste

Brown ground beef with diced peppers and onion. Drain well. Place ground beef mixture in crockpot. Toss diced potato with melted butter to coat and add to crockpot; add whole kernel corn and creamed corn. Salt and pepper to taste. Cover and cook on low for 7 to 9 hours. Taste and adjust seasonings. Serves 4 to 6.

CROCKPOT CHOCOLATE APPLE CAKE
    6 tbsp butter
    1/2 c sugar
    1/2 c brown sugar
    1 c unsweetened applesauce
    1 tsp cinnamon
    1 tsp pure vanilla extract
    3 eggs
    4 (1 oz) sq unsweetened chocolate, melted
    1 1/2 c flour
    2 tsp baking soda
    1 tsp baking powder
    pinch of salt
    1/3 c buttermilk
    3/4 c semisweet chocolate chips
    1/2 c chopped pecans
    Confectioner's sugar
In a large bowl, beat together butter & sugars w/a mixer on HIGH speed 1-2 minutes, or until fluffy. Beat in applesauce, cinnamon, vanilla & eggs until well mixed. Beat in melted chocolate until blended. Add flour, baking soda & powder, & salt. With mixer on LOW speed, beat in dry ingredients, adding buttermilk as you beat. Beat just until evenly mixed. By hand stir in chocolate chips & pecans. Scrape the
      batter into a WELL BUTTERED 3 1/2 quart crockpot & smooth top. Cover & cook on the HIGH setting 2 1/4 to 2 1/2 hrs, or until a cake tester (toothpick) inserted in the center comes out clean. (Do not cook on the low heat setting for a longer time) Remove lid & let cake stand in crockpot until just barely warm. To unmold: Run a sharp knife around the inside edges of the crockpot & w/a large spatula, carefully lift out the cake in one piece. Sprinkle with confectioner's sugar over top & cut into wedges to serve.

CROCKPOT CHOCOLATE APPLE SAUCE CAKE
    6 Tbsp butter

1 cup sugar
1 cup unsweetened applesauce
1 tsp cinnamon
1 tsp vanilla
3 eggs
4 (1 oz) squares unsweetened chocolate, melted
1 1/2 cups flour
2 tsp baking soda
1 tsp baking powder
pinch of salt
1/3 cup buttermilk
3/4 cup semisweet chocolate chips
1/2 cup chopped walnuts
powdered sugar

-In a large bowl, beat together the butter and sugar w/a mixer on high speed 1-2 minutes, or until fluffy. Beat in the applesauce, cinnamon, vanilla and eggs until well mixed. Beat in the melted choclate until blended. Add the flour, baking soda & powder, and salt. With the mixer on low speed, beat in the dry ingredients, adding the buttermilk as you beat. Beat just until evenly mixed. By hand, stir in chocolate chips and nuts. Scrape the batter into a WELL BUTTERED 3 1/2 quart slow cooker (crock pot) and smooth the top.

-Cover and cook on the high setting 2 1/4 to 2 1/2 hours, or until a cake tester inserted in the center comes out clean. (Do not cook on the low heat setting for a longer time)

-Remove the lid and let the cake stand in the slow cooker until just barely warm.

To unmold, run a sharp knife around the inside edges of the crock and w/a large spatula, carefully lift out the cake in one piece. Sprinkle with powdered sugar over the top and cut into wedges to serve.

CROCKPOT CHOCOLATE CLUSTERS

* 2 pounds white almond bark
* 4 ounces bar German chocolate
* 1 pkg. semi-sweet chocolate chips (12 ounces)
* 24 ounces dry roasted peanuts

Put all ingredients in Crock Pot; cover and cook on high for 1 hour. Do not stir. Turn Crock Pot to low and stir every 15 minutes for

1 hour. Drop on waxed paper and let cool. Store in a tightly covered container.

CROCKPOT CHOCOLATE PEANUT BUTTER CAKE

    2 c. chocolate cake mix
    1/2 c. water
    1/3 c. creamy peanut butter
    1/2 c. chopped nuts

Combine all ingredients in bowl mixing well. Beat about 2 minutes. Pour batter into greased and floured 2 pound coffee can. Place can in crockpot. Cover top of can with 8 paper towels. Cover crockpot and bake on high 2 to 3 hours.

CROCKPOT CHOPS OR RIBS

    6 or 8 chops or ribs to fill CP (I made less)
    1/4 C chopped onion
    1/2 C chopped celery
    1 C catsup
    1/2 C water
    1/4 C lemon juice
    2 Tbsp brown sugar
    3 Tbsp Worcestershire sauce
    2 Tbsp vinegar
    1 Tbsp mustard
    1/2 tsp salt
    1/4 tsp pepper

Mix together & pour over meat in pot. Cook until tender.

Note: Actually, I left out the onion & celery (didn't have any) but put some cut up carrots in the bottom of the CP, then the pork chops & then the marinade. It tasted very good. I think I cooked it for 1 hour on high & then about 4 hours on low....my chops were frozen when I put them in.

CROCKPOT CHOW MEIN

    4 oz. can mushrooms
    1 1/2 lbs. cubed round steak
    4 stocks celery
    2 med. onions

1 c. hot water with 3 bouillon cubes
3 tbsp. soy sauce
2 tsp. Worcestershire sauce
1 lb. can Chinese vegetables
2 tbsp. cornstarch and 2 tbsp. water
Cook 8 to 10 hours in crockpot - 1 hour before serving add Chinese vegetables and cornstarch and water.

CROCKPOT CHUNKY VEGETABLE CLAM CHOWDER

2 6 1/2 oz cans minced clams
2 c. peeled potatoes, cut into 1/2" cubes
1 c. finely chopped onion
1 c. chopped celery
1 tsp. sugar
1/4 tsp. salt
1/4 tsp. pepper
2 10 3/4 oz cans condensed cream of potato soup
2 c. water
1 c. nonfat dry milk powder
1/3 c. flour
1 c. cold water
4 slices bacon, crisp-cooked, drained, and crumbled
Paprika

Drain clams, reserving liquid. Cover clams; chill. In CP combine reserved clam liquid, potatoes, onion, celery, carrot, sugar, salt, and papper. Stir in potato sour and 2 cups water. Cover; cook on low heat for 8 to 10 hours or on high heat for 4 to 5 hours. If using low heat setting, turn to high. In a medium bowl combine nonfat dry milk powder and flour. Gradually whisk in 1 c. cold water; stir into soup. Cover; cook on high 10 to 15 minutes or till thickened. Stir in clams. Cover; cook 5 minutes more. Ladle soup into bowls. Sprinkle each serving with crumbled bacon and paprika. Makes 6 to 8 servings.

CROCKPOT CLAM CHOWDER I

4 cans of Cream of Potato soup
4 cans of New England Clam Chowder
2 cans minced clams with juice

1 onion, chopped and sauteed in
1 stick butter
1 quart half and half
Saute onions in butter, then add all ingredients in crockpot for 4 hours... I usually put it on low and cook it all day... Also it makes alot and sometimes over fills my crockpot.. Dont know if its my crockpot being too small or just too much stuff LOL .. Im sure if you wanted you could cut the ingredients in half ... ENJOY!!

CROCKPOT CLAM CHOWDER II
   * 4 (6 1/2 oz.) cans clams
   * 1/2 lb. salt pork or bacon, diced
   * 1 lg. onion, chopped
   * 6 to 8 lg. potatoes, pared and cubed
   * 3 c. water
   * 3 1/2 tsp. salt
   * 1/4 tsp. pepper
   * 4 c. half and half cream or milk
   * 3 to 4 tbsp. cornstarch

Cut clams into bite sized pieces if necessary. In skillet, saute salt pork or bacon and onion until golden brown; drain. Put into Crock Pot with clams. Add all remaining ingredients, except milk. Cover; cook on high 3 to 4 hours or until potatoes are tender. During the last hour of cooking, combine 1 cup of milk with the cornstarch. Add that and the remaining milk and stir well; heat through. Serve in large bowls with crusty French bread.

CROCKPOT COBBLER
All you do is bake a batch of biscuits and let them cool. Chunk them up and put about half in the bottom of your crockpot.
   Mix:
   1/4 cup brown sugar
   1/2 t. cinnamon
   1/2 cup butter
Sprinkle some of that on top. Spread canned pie filling (I thought cherry would be good) on top and repeat until you're out of ingredients. Bake on high for 2 hours.

CROCKPOT COCONUT THAI SHRIMP AND RICE

2 (10 oz.) cans chicken broth
1 cup water
1 tsp. coriander
1/2 tsp. cumin
1 tsp salt
1/2 tsp cayenne pepper
zest and juice of 2 limes (1/3 cup of juice)
7 cloves minced garlic
1 TBLSP. minced fresh ginger
1 medium onion chopped
1 red bell pepper chopped
1 carrott peeled and shredded
1/4 cup flaked coconut
1/2 cup golden raisins
2 cups converted rice
1 lb. peeled and deveined jumbo cooking shrimp (thawed if frozen)
2 oz. fresh snow peas cut into strips
toasted coconut for garnish (optional)

In a 5 qt cp, combine chicken broth, water, coriander, cumin, salt, cayenne pepper, lime zest, lime juice, garlic and ginger. Stir in onion, pepper, carrot, coconut, raisins and rice.

Cover and cook on low 3 1/2 hours, or until rice is tender. Check after 3 hours and if liquid is absorbed, but rice is not tender, add 1 more cup water. When rice is tender, stir in shrimp and snow peas. Cook 30 minutes longer. Sprinkle with toasted coconut and serve.

CROCKPOT COLA BARBECUE PORK ROAST

1 pork roast
1 1/2 cup cola
1 bottle bbq sauce

Cut all visible fat from roast,put in crock and cook 12 hrs (i put mine in before bed and let cook all night) on low. Remove meat from crock and drain all juice from crock. Shred meat and return to crock add 1 bottle bbq sauce and cook 5-6 hrs more.

MAKES ALOT!!! Freezes great.

CROCKPOT COLA HAM

1/2 cup brown sugar
1 tsp dry mustard
1/4 cup cola (Coca Cola(r), Pepsi, etc)
3 to 4 pound pre-cooked ham

Combine brown sugar and mustard. Moisten with cola to make a smooth paste. Reserve remaining cola. Score the ham with shallow slashes in a diamond pattern. Rub ham with mixture. Place ham in crockpot and add remaining cola. Cover and cook on high for 1 hour, then turn to low and cook for 6 to 7 hours. Serves 9 to 12.

CROCKPOT COQ AU VIN

12 sm White onions, peeled
4 lb Roasting chicken, cut up
1/2 ts Salt
1/4 ts Black pepper
1/4 c Brandy or cognac
2 ea Cloves garlic, peeled and crushed
1/4 ts Ground thyme
1 ea Bay leaf
1 1/2 c Dry, strong red wine
5 tb All purpose flour
1 c Chicken bouillon
3/4 lb Fresh mushrooms, wiped and stemmed
1 tb Butter or margarine
1/4 ts Salt
1 tb Chopped fresh parsley

To cook: Place the onions in the slow cooker. Remove the fat from the vent of the chicken and dice it. In a large skillet over medium heat, heat the fat until it is rendered. Discard the shriveled bits and saute the chicken until well browned. Season with 1/2 tsp salt and the pepper. Warm the brandy in a ladle or a small saucepan; light it with match and pour it over the chicken. When the flame dies, lift the chicken into the slow cooker and add the garlic, thyme, and bay leaf.

Pour the wine into the hot skillet and scrape up the pan juices. Dissolve the flour in the bouillon, turn it into the skillet and bring to simmering, stirring briskly to prevent lumps. Turn into the slow cooker. Cover and cook on Low 7-9 hours. Before serving: About 10 minutes before serving, in a medium skillet, saute the mushrooms in the butter over medium high heat. In about 5 minutes, they will be tender and the moisture will have evaporated from the skillet. Season with 1/4 tsp salt and add to the chicken casserole. If the sauce seems thin, simmer it in the mushroom skillet long enough to thicken to the consistency of heavy cream. Garnish the Coq au Vin with parsley before serving.

CROCKPOT COQ AU VIN

2-1/2 lb chicken cut up (I used boneless, skinless chicken breasts)
1 clove garlic crushed
1 teaspoon salt
1/4 teaspoon pepper
1/2 teaspoon dried thyme
6 bacon slices, diced
2/3 cups sliced green onions
1 cup chicken broth
8 small white onions, peeled
1 cup burgundy wine
1/2 LB whole mushrooms
chopped parsley
8 small new potatoes scrubbed

In large skillet, saute dieced bacon and green onions until bacon is crisp. Remove and drain on paper towel. Add chicken pieces to skillet and brown well on all sides. Remove the chicken when it has browned and set aside. Put peeled onions, mushrooms, and garlic in Crockpot. Add browned chicken pieces, bacon and green onions, salt, pepper, thyme, pototales and chicken broth. Cover and cook on Low 6 -

8 hours (High 3-4). During the last hour add Burgundy and cook on high. Garnish with chopped parsley.

CROCKPOT COQ AU VIN WITH SHIITAKE MUSHROOMS

2 tbs. olive oil
3 lb. chicken pieces, rinsed & patted dry
1/3 c finely chopped shallot
1/3 c finely chopped onion
2 carrots, quartered lengthwise & cut crosswise into 1/4" pieces (about 1/2 cup)
1/2 lb. pearl onions, blanched in boiling water for 3 minutes, drained, & peeled
1 bay leaf
3/4 tsp thyme, crumbled
2 tbs. Cognac
1 c dry white wine
2 c chicken broth
1/4 lb. shiitake mushrooms, stems discarded & caps sliced thin
1/4 c cornstarch
Freshly ground nutmeg to taste

-In a heavy kettle, heat the oil over moderately high heat until it is hot but not smoking and in it saute the chicken pieces, seasoned with salt and pepper, in batches, turning them once, for 8 to 10 minutes, or until they are browned. Transfer the chicken pieces as they are browned to a plate and keep them warm, covered. -Place the shallot, onions, carrots, pearl onions, bay leaf, and thyme in a crockpot. Place the browned chicken on top of the vegetables. Combine the Cognac, white wine and 1 3/4 cup of chicken broth and add to the cooker. Cover and cook on LOW for 5 hours or until chicken is tender.

-Turn control to HIGH and add the mushrooms. Dissolve the cornstarch in the remaining 1/4 cup chicken stock. Stir into the mixture. Cover and cook for 20 minutes more, or until sauce is thickened, stirring once. Transfer the chicken to a plate, and keep warm. Discard the bay leaf, and season the sauce with freshly ground nutmeg and salt and pepper to taste. Serve warm.
Serves 4 to 5

CROCKPOT CORN CHOWDER I

6 slices bacon, diced
1/2 c. chopped onion

2 c. diced peeled potatoes
2 pkgs. (10 oz each) frozen whole-kernel corn, broken apart
1 can (16 oz) cream-style corn
1 Tbs. sugar
1 tsp. Worcestershire sauce
1 tsp. seasoned salt
1/4 tsp. pepper
1 c. water

In skillet, fry bacon until crisp; remove and reserve. Add onion and potatoes to bacon drippings and saute for about 5 minutes; drain well. Combine all ingredients in CP; stir well. Cover and cook on Low setting for 4 to 7 hours. Makes about 1 ½ quarts.

CROCKPOT CORN CHOWDER II

3 16oz cans of corn, drained
2 large potatoes, cut into 1" chunks
1 & 1/2 can chicken broth*
1 large onion, diced
1 tsp.. salt
pepper to taste
2 pints half and half*
1/2 stick butter
*adjust volume somewhat lower for thicker chowder

Put everything except the dairy products in the crockpot and cook on low for 7-8 hours. Remove to a blender, and puree. Return to crockpot, add half & half and butter; stir. Cook on high for one hour. Stir and serve. Serves six.

CROCKPOT CORN PUDDING

8 oz. cream cheese, softened
2 eggs, beaten
1/3 cup sugar
8 1/2 oz package corn bread mix
16 oz can cream style corn
2 1/3 cups frozen sweet corn
1 cup milk
2 tablespoons margarine, melted
1 tsp. salt

1/4 tsp nutmeg
Lightly grease CP. In a bowl, blend cream cheese, eggs and sugar. Add remaining ingredients and mix well. Pour into CP. Cover and cook on High 3 to 4 hours. Serves 10 to 12

CROCKPOT CORNED BEEF AND CABBAGE
Yield: 6 servings
4 1/2 lb. Corned beef brisket
2 md onions, quartered
1 cabbage head, cut in small wedges
1/2 tsp. pepper
3 tbsp. vinegar
3 tbsp. sugar
2 c. water
Combine ingredients in removable liner with cabbage on top. Cut meat to fit, if necessary. Place liner in base. Cover and cook on low 10-12 hours, high 6-7 hours, or auto 6-8 hours.

CROCKPOT CORNED BEEF AND CABBAGE
3 lb uncooked corned beef brisket (in pouch with pickling juice is okay)
2 carrots, chopped into 2" pieces
5 small red potatoes, halved
1 onion, quartered
1 small turnip, chopped into 2" pieces
3/4 cup malt vinegar
1/2 bottle (6 oz) Irish stout (Guiness?)
1 tsp mustard seed
1 tsp coriander seed
1 tsp black peppercorns (whole)
1 tsp dill seed
1 tsp allspice (whole)
1 bay leaf
1 small (2 Lb) head cabbage, cut into wedges
In a LARGE (6.5 qt) Crock-Pot, place the carrots, spuds, onion and turnip in bottom. Add the liquids. Spice rub the brisket. Place on top. Cover and cook on LOW for 8 hours. Add cabbage wedges. Cook an additional 3 hours on LOW. Serve with Coarse Grain Mustard and Horseradish Sauce.

-Horseradish Sauce:
1/2 pint whipping cream
3 Tbsp prepared horseradish
Whip cream until it peaks, then fold in horseradish.

CROCKPOT CORNED BEEF HASH I
1 can of corned beef (Or 2 cups of cooked corned beef)
1 med onion shredded
2 med. celery sticks chopped
5 fair sized potatoes chopped
2 tbsp. butter
1 diced green pepper
garlic to your taste (I use about 3 cloves or so)
1 cup mushrooms (I omit this now since my daughter has decided they are gross) LOL
1 tbsp of worcestshire sauce
a dash or two of italian seasoning
salt and pepper to taste
2- 10 oz cans of chicken broth
-Grind up or chop your corned beef and toss it in the crock pot with all the other ingredients in the list above.
-Cook in your crock pot on low for 8 hours. When the potatoes are well cooked I mash them in the pot and add a little water if need be. Then serve it with warm bread and salad!

CROCKPOT CORNED BEEF HASH II
1 tin of corned beef hash
3 BIG potatoes
3 ribs of celery chopped
1 large onion chopped
2 big cloves of garlic
salt and pepper to taste
a dash or so of basil
2 tins of chicken broth
-Fry the Garlic, celery, onion, and salt and pepper in a tbsp of garlic til veggies are tender.
-Then toss everything in the crock pot and turn on low for about 5-6 hours.

-Serve with lots of warm bread and butter.

CROCKPOT CORNY HAM AND POTATO SCALLOP
5 potatoes, peeled and cubed
1 1/2 cups cubed cooked ham
1 (15 ounce) can whole kernel corn, drained
1/4 cup chopped green bell pepper
2 teaspoons instant minced onion
1 (11 ounce) can condensed cheddar cheese soup
1/2 cup milk
3 tablespoons all-purpose flour
In a 3 1/2 to 4 quart slow cooker, combine potatoes, ham, corn, green pepper and onion; mix well. In a small bowl, combine soup, milk and flour; beat with wire whisk until smooth. Pour soup mixture over potato mixture and stir gently to mix. Cover and cook on low setting for about 8 hours or until potatoes are tender.

CROCKPOT COSTA RICAN BEEF & VEGETABLE SOUP WITH YELLOW RICE
Yield: 6 servings
2 lb Lean, boneless beef chuck in 1 1/2 inch cubes
1 lg Onion, thinly sliced
1 c Celery, thinly sliced
3 Cloves garlic, minced
1 Dry bay leaf
1 lg Red bell pepper, seeded and cut into thin, bite-size strips
1 1/2 c Water
2 Cans (about 14 1/2 oz.@) Beef broth
YELLOW RICE
1 lg Ear corn, cut into 3/4 inch thick slices
4 c Coarsely shredded cabbage
1/3 c Lightly packed cilantro leaves
Salt and pepper
THE SOUP: Arrange beef cubes slightly apart in a single layer in a shallow baking pan. Bake in a 500 oven until well browned (about 20 minutes). Meanwhile, in a 3 1/2 quart or larger crockpot, combine onion, celery, garlic, bay leaf and bell pepper. Transfer browned beef to crockpot. Pour a little of the water into baking pan, stirring to

dissolve drippings and pour into crockpot. Add broth and remaining water. Cover and cook on low about 8 hours. About 15 minutes before beef is done, prepare Yellow Rice. While rice is cooking, increase cooker setting to high; add corn. Cover; cook for 5 minutes. Add cabbage; cover and cook until cabbage is bright green, 8 to 10 more minutes. Stir in cilantro; season with salt and pepper. Ladle soup into wide, shallow bowls; add a scoop of rice to each.

THE RICE:
1 tablespoon salad oil
1 small onion, finely chopped
1 cup long-grain white rice
1/4 teaspoon ground turmeric
1 3/4 cups water

Heat oil in 2-quart pan over medium heat. Add the onion; cook, stirring until onion is soft but not browned, (3 to 5 minutes). Stir in the rice and tumeric; cook, stirring occasionally, for about 1 minute. Pour in the water and reduce heat to low and cook until rice is tender, about 20 minutes.

CROCKPOT COUNTRY CHICKEN STEW WITH BASIL DUMPLINGS

12 small white onions
water
1 pound boneless skinless chicken thighs
1 pound bonless skinless chicken breasts halves
1/2 Tablespoon chopped fresh basil leaves
(or 1/2 teaspoon dried, crumbled)
salt and pepper to taste
1 large red bell pepper cut into 1" squares
4 cloves garlic - thinly sliced
2 cups canned chicken broth
1/3 cup dry white wine
2 Tablesppons all purpose flour
2 Tablespoon butter - room temperature
1 pound fres asparagus - cut into 1-1/2" lengths
DUMPLINGS:
1 cup buttermilk and baking mix
1/3 cup whole milk

1/4 cup chopped fresh basil leaves (or 1 Tablespoon dried, crumbled)

1. Using a sharp knife, make a small X in the root end of each onion. Bring a saucepan of water to boil. Add the onions, lower the heat, and simmer for 5 minutes. Drain and rinse under running cold water. Slip skins off onions.

2. Rinse chicken and pat dry. Quarter the thighs and chicken breast halves. Stir in basil and seaons with salt and pepper.

3. Put chicken pieces in a 3-1/2 quart or larger crockery slow-cooker. Top with onions, bell peppers, and garlic. Pour in stock, and wine. DO NOT sitr. Cover and cook on LOW for 6 - 8 hours or HIGH for 2 - 2-1/2 hours.

4. Stir the stew. If cooking on LOW, change setting to HIGH. In a small bowl, blend together the flour and butter. Stir into slow-cooker. cook, stirring until sauce begins to thicken, about 5 minutes. Stir in asparagus.

5. In medium bowl, combine dumpling ingredients until evenly moistened. Drop by Tablespoons onto hot stew in 6 small rounds. Cover and cook for another 25 to 30 minutes, until dumplings are cooked through. Serve immediately!

CROCKPOT COUNTRY STYLE RIBS AND KRAUT
12 oz sauerkraut
brown sugar to taste
1-2 lbs country style ribs
Place the ribs in a crockpot. Sweeten the sauerkraut to taste with the brown sugar.

Cook them all day while at work and come home to tender and delicious ribs and kraut. Mash a potato and dinner is ready!

CROCKPOT CRANAPPLE SAUCE
10-12 medium apples
1-2 cups cranberry juice
lemon juice -- use 1/4 to 1/2 lemon
2 tbs sugar -- or up to 1/4 cup if you want it sweet
1/4 to 1/2 cup dried cranberries or "craisins" (sweetened dried cranberries)

-Wash the apples and chop them up without peeling. Squeeze lemon juice over them as you cut them.

-Put apples in crockpot with cranberry juice -- use 1 cup if you want the applesauce thick, more if you want it thin. Stir in sugar to suit your taste.

-Let apples stew on low for 6-8 hours. About an hour or two before serving, stir in cranberries or craisins. (All I found at my store was craisins--since they're sweetened, I used less sugar.)

-The applesauce is a very pretty pink and the cranberries & juice give it a nice zing.

-As you can see, the recipe is simple and forgiving -- let the apples stew a little longer or a little less -- the longer you stew them the mushier the applesauce will be. It warms up nicely, or you can eat it cold.

CROCKPOT CRANBERRIES
   * 1 pkg. fresh cranberries
   * 2 c. sugar
   * 1/4 c. water

Combine cranberries with sugar and water in Crock Pot. Cover and cook on high 2 to 3 hours until some pop. Serve with turkey or chicken.

CROCKPOT CRANBERRY CHICKEN
   1 small onion, thinly sliced
   1 cup fresh or frozen (unthawed) cranberries
   12 skinless, boneless chicken thgihs (about 2 1/4 lbs. total)
   1/4 cup catsup
   2 tablespoons firmly packed brown sugar
   1 teaspoon dry mustard
   2 teaspoons cider vinegar 1 1/2 tablespoons cornstarch blended w/2 tablespoons cold
   water
   salt

-In a 3-quart or larger electric slow cooker, combine onion, cranberries. Arrange chicken on top. In small bowl, mix catsup, sugar, mustard and vinegar and pour over chicken. Cover. Cook at low setting until chicken is very tender when pierced (6 1/2 to 7 1/2 hours).

-Lift out chicken when done, blend cornstarch mixture into cooking liquid. Increase cooker heat setting to high; cover and cook, stirring 2 or 3 times until sauce thickens (10 to 15 more minutes). Season to taste with salt; pour over chicken.

Makes 6 servings.

-REAL WORLD COOKING: I cooked at a higher heat setting than they did because I was in a hurry. I also did not remove the chicken, just threw the cornstarch in and stirred it in and then cranked up the heat a bit. Didn't stir again more than once. Then dumped it onto a big platter. It was fine. I also chose to use 7 chicken breasts instead of the 12 thighs. It also didn't take as long as 6 1/2 hours.

CROCKPOT CRANBERRY PORK

1 (16 ounce) can cranberry sauce
1/3 cup French salad dressing
1 onion, sliced
3 pounds pork roast

In a medium bowl, combine the cranberry sauce, salad dressing and onions. Place pork in a slow cooker and pour the sauce over the pork. Cook on high setting for 4 hours OR on low setting for 8 hours. Pork is done when its internal temperature has reached 160°F (70°C).

CROCKPOT CRANBERRY PORK ROAST

Serves: 4 to 6
4 medium potatoes, peeled and cut into 1" chunks
One 3-pound boneless center-cut pork loin roast, rolled and tied
1 can (16 ounces) whole-berry cranberry sauce
1 can (5.5 ounces) apricot nectar
1 medium onion, coarsely chopped
1/2 cup coarsely chopped dried apricots
1/2 cup sugar
1 teaspoon dry mustard
1/4 teaspoon crushed red pepper

Place the potatoes in a 3 1/2-quart (or larger) slow cooker, then place the roast over the potatoes. In a large bowl, combine the remaining ingredients; mix well and pour over the roast. Cover and cook on the low setting for 5 to 6 hours. Remove the roast to a cutting board and thinly slice. Serve with the potatoes and sauce.

CROCKPOT CRAZY STANDING UP PORK CHOPS

Yield: 4 servings
4 Loin pork chops -- lean
2 md Onions -- sliced
1 ts Butter
Salt & Pepper -- to taste
Spices of your choice

Stand chops in crockpot, thin side down. Sprinkle with salt, pepper and spices of your choice. Cover with the onion slices, which have been separated into rings. Place butter on top, and cook on LOW heat for 6 to 8 hours, or until chops are tender and onions are done. The result is moist, tender chops with a deep brown color as if broiled in the oven.

CROCKPOT CREAM CHEESE CHICKEN

1 frying chicken -- cut up
2 tablespoons melted butter or margarine
salt & pepper -- to taste
2 tablespoons dry Italian salad dressing
1 can condensed mushroom soup
6 ounces cream cheese; -- cut in 1" cubes
1/2 cup sauterne wine or sherry
1 tablespoon onion -- minced

Brush chicken with butter and sprinkle with salt and pepper. Place in a crockpot and sprinkle dry mix over all. Cover and cook on low for 6 - 7 hours. About 45 minutes before done, mix soup, cream cheese, wine, and onion in a small saucepan. Cook until smooth. Pour over the chicken and cover and cook another 45 minutes.

Serve with sauce.

CROCKPOT CREAM OF SWEET POTATO SOUP

3 Sweet potatoes, peeled and sliced
2 c Chicken bouillon

1 ts Sugar
1/8 ts Each ground cloves and nutmeg
Salt to taste
1 1/2 c Light cream, half-and-half, or milk
Put sweet potatoes and bouillon in cooker. Cover and cook on high 2 to 3 hours or until potatoes are tender. Force potatoes and liquid through food mill or puree in blender. Put back in cooker with remaining ingredients. Cover and cook on high 1 to 2 hours. Serve hot or chilled with a dollop of sour cream if desired. Makes about 1 quart.

CROCKPOT CREAMY CHICKEN DINNER
4 boneless/skinless chicken breasts seasoned with garlic powder, onion powder and
season salt
1 large can cream of chicken soup
2 cans cream of mushroom soup
3/4 c frozen cut carrots
3/4 c frozen green beans
Dump it all in the crockpot and cook it about 7 hours on low. Add 2 cups of minute rice to it the last 5 minutes before dinner.

CROCKPOT CREAMY HASH BROWNS
1 2-lb pkg frozen cubed hash brown potatoes
8 oz shredded or cubed Velveeta
16 oz sour cream
1 can cream of celery soup
1 can cream of chicken soup
1 lb bacon, cooked & crumbled
1 lg onion, chopped (I omitted this)
1/4 C butter or margarine, melted
1/4 tsp pepper (I used alot more and also added some salt)
Place potatoes in an ungreased crockpot. In a bowl, combine the remaining ingredients. Pour over potatoes and mix well. Cover and cook on low for 4-5 hours (until potatoes are tender and heated through).
You can serve it with biscuits and fruit salad.

CROCKPOT CREAMY ORANGE CHEESECAKE

Crust:
3/4 cup cookie or graham cracker crumbs
2 tablespoons sugar
3 tablespoons melted butter
Filling:
16 ounces cream cheese (light)
2/3 cup sugar
2 eggs
1 egg yolk
1/4 cup frozen orange juice concentrate, thawed
1 teaspoon orange or lemon zest, or dried grated rind
1 tablespoon flour
1/2 teaspoon vanilla
-Combine crumbs with sugar; mix in melted butter until well moistened. Pat into a
7-inch springform pan.
-In a medium bowl, cream together the cream cheese and sugar. Add eggs and yolk and
beat for about 3 minutes on medium with a hand-held electric mixer. Beat in orange juice, zest, flour, and vanilla. Beat for another 2 minutes. Pour batter into prepared crust; place on a rack or aluminum foil ring in the crockery cooker (so it doesn't rest on the bottom of the pot). Cover and cook on high for 2 1/2 to 3 hours. Turn off and leave for 1 to 2 hours, until cool enough to remove. Cool completely and remove the sides of the pan. Chill before serving, and store leftovers in the refrigerator.

CROCKPOT CREAMY RED POTATOES

2 lbs small red potatoes, quartered
2 (8 oz) pkgs. cream cheese, softened
1 can cream of potato soup, undiluted
1 envelope rance salad dressing mix
Place potatoes in crockpot. In a small bowl, beat cream cheese, soup and salad dressing, mix. Stir into potatoes. Cover and cook on low for 8 hours or until potatoes are tender. Also add about a tablespoon of milk.

CROCKPOT CREAMY SPINACH NOODLE CASSEROLE

Served alongside baked or roasted chicken, this delicious side dish will please every person at your dinner table. Feel free to use low-fat sour cream and cottage cheese or increase the amount of hot sauce! Makes approximately 5 side servings.

8 ounces dry spinach noodles
2 tbsp. vegetable oil
1 1/2 cups sour cream
1/3 cup all-purpose flour
1 1/2 cups cottage cheese
4 green onions, minced
2 tsp. Worcestershire sauce
1 dash hot pepper sauce
2 tsp. garlic salt

-Cook noodles in a pot of salted, boiling water until just tender. Drain and rinse with cold water. Toss with vegetable oil.

-Combine sour cream and flour in a large bowl, mixing well. Stir in cottage cheese, green onions, Worcestershire sauce, hot pepper sauce and garlic salt. Fold noodles into mixture until well combined.

-Generously grease the inside of a slow cooker and pour in noodle mixture. Cover and cook on high for 1 1/2 to 2 hours.

CROCKPOT CREOLE BLACK BEANS

1 to 2 pounds Smoked sausage, cut into 1" slices
3 15 oz cans black beans, drained
1 1/2 cups Onions -- chopped
1 1/2 cups Green pepper, chopped
1 1/2 cups Celery, chopped
3 cloves Garlic, minced
2 teaspoons Leaf thyme
1 1/2 teaspoons Leaf oregano
1 1/2 teaspoons White pepper
1/4 teaspoon Black pepper
1/4 teaspoon Cayenne pepper
1 Chicken bouillon cube
5 Bay leaves
1 can 8-oz. tomato sauce
1 cup Water
Hot boiled rice

-Brown sausage in a skillet over med. heat. Drain fat and transfer to crockpot.

Combine remaining ingredients in crockpot. Cover and cook on low 8 hrs. or on high 4 hrs. Remove bay leaves. Serve over cooked rice. Serves 6 to 8.

CROCKPOT CREOLE CHICKEN
8 chicken thighs (I used 3 big breasts)
1 can diced tomatoes (I used 1 can whole tomatoes chopped up)
1 can tomato paste (I used 1 can Rotel drained)
1 chopped bell pepper
1 chopped onion chopped ham (I used one thick slice ham chopped up)
diced sausage (I left this out only because I didn't have any)
Tabasco sauce to taste (I left this out)
-Throw it all in the crock and cook on low 4-5 hours. I thickened it a little at the end with cornstarch. I served it over brown rice. The ham gave it really good flavor. We really liked it.

CROCKPOT CRYSTAL'S LEFTOVER PORK ROAST CASSEROLE
1 package cooked noodles (any type is fine)
1 package beans (any type is fine)
Beef Boullion
1 package long grain and wild rice (I prefer Uncle Ben's)
3 potatoes, cut into 1" cubes
Leftover pork from your roast (or any other leftover meat really!)
Salt and Pepper to taste -Fill your crockpot a little more than half way with water, then flavor it with the beef boullion to taste. Add the sliced up potatoes, beans and rice. Cook until potatoes and rice are done, most of the day on low or half of the day on high. Add the pork and let that cook while you boil the noodles. Add the noodles to the pot
when they're done. Let cook for 5 to 10 more minutes and serve.

CROCKPOT CUSTARD

3 eggs, lightly beaten
1/3 cup sugar
1 teaspoon vanilla
2 cups milk
1/4 teaspoon ground nutmeg

In a mixing bowl combine eggs, sugar, vanilla and milk; mix well. Pour into a lightly buttered 1- or 1 1/2-quart baking dish or souffle which will fit in the slow cooker/Crock Pot, and sprinkle with the nutmeg. Place a rack or ring of aluminum foil in the slow cooker/Crock Pot, then add 1 1/2 to 2 cups of hot water to the pot. Cover the baking dish with aluminum foil and place on the rack in the slow cooker/Crock Pot. Cover and cook on high for 2 1/2 to 3 hours, or until set.

Serves 4 to 6.

CROCKPOT DRESSING
1 (8 inch) pan cornbread
8 slices dry white bread
4 eggs
2 c. chicken broth
2 cans cream of chicken soup
1 tsp. sage
1/2 tsp. black pepper
Celery to taste
1 med. onion
2 tbsp. butter

Mix ingredients except butter. Place in crock pot. Dot butter on top. Cook 2 hours on High then 4 hours on low.

CROCKPOT FRUIT DESSERT
* 3 Grapefruit, peeled
* sectioned
* 1 can (11 oz) mandarin orange, sections, drained
* 1 can (16 oz) fruit cocktail, well drained
* 1 can (20 oz) pineapple chunks, well drained
* 1 can (16 oz) sliced peaches, well drained
* 3 Bananas, sliced
* 1 tablespoon Lemon juice
* 1 can (21 oz) cherry pie filling

Place all ingredients in cooker. Toss gently. Cover and cook on low about 4 hours.

Makes about 2 quarts.

CROCKPOT HAMBURGER CASSEROLE

2 lbs. browned ground beef
3 carrots, peeled and sliced
2 onions, sliced
4 potatoes, peeled and sliced
1 can peas, drained
2 stalks celery, diced
1 can cream of chicken soup
1 can water

Place potatoes in bottom of crockpot, top with carrots and other vegetables. Place

ground beef on top. Combine soup and water and pour over ground beef. Cover and cook on low for 6 to 8 hours.

CROCKPOT HAMBURGER-SAUSAGE DIP

* 1 pound ground chuck
* 1 cup picante sauce
* 1 can cream of mushroom soup
* 2 pound Velveeta cheese...cut into pieces
* 1 pound pork sausage
* 1 teaspoon garlic powder
* 1 can Rotel tomatoes
* 3/4 teaspoon oregano

Combine picante sauce, garlic powder, soup, tomatoes, oregano and cheese in Crock Pot. Brown ground chuck and sausage until it is done. Drain very well and place in slow cooker/Crock Pot. Cook on low until cheese is melted. Serve with your favorite chips.

CROCKPOT HOT DIP

* 1 pound Italian Sausage - hot
* 1 pounds velveeta - Mexican type - hot
* 1 can rotel tomatoes (drained)
* 1 jar pace picante sauce - hot
* 1 jalapeno pepper - finely diced
- -Brown sausage and drain along with jalapeno pepper.

- -Add to slow cooker/Crock Pot with other ingredients and simmer on low for 1 hour
or more until melted and blended.
- -Serve with tortilla strips or chips, large Fritos corn chips, or even lightly toasted and cubed sourdough bread.

CROCKPOT JAMBALAYA
* 1 pound Chicken breasts, boneless
* - cut in 1" cubes
* 1 pound Smoked sausage, sliced
* 1 pound Shrimp, cooked
* 28 ounces Crushed tomatoes
* 1 md Onion, chopped
* 1 Green pepper, chopped
* 1 cup Chicken broth
* 1/2 cup White wine
* 2 teaspoons Oregano
* 2 teaspoons Parsley
* 2 teaspoons Cajun seasoning
* 1 teaspoon Cayenne pepper
* 2 cups Rice, cooked

Cut chicken and slice sausage. Chop onion and green pepper. Put all in slow cooker/Crock Pot. Add remaining ingredients, except shrimp and rice. Cook in slow cooker/Crock Pot on low for 6-8 hours. 30 minutes before eating, add cooked shrimp and cooked rice; allow to heat.
Can be cooked on high for 3-4 hours instead.

CROCKPOT LASAGNA
1 pkg. pepperoni slices
1 lb. hamburger
1 onion, diced
1 green pepper, diced
1 can mushrooms
1 pkg. kluski noodles
1 lg. jar pizza sauce
1 lg. jar spaghetti sauce
1 pkg. each shredded Colby & Mozzarella cheese

Cook together hamburger, onion, green pepper and mushrooms. Layer this with the rest of the ingredients in the crock pot. Cook on high for 2 to 3 hours.

CROCKPOT LITTLE SMOKIES
* 2 packages Cocktail wieners
* 1 Medium bottle chili sauce
* 1 Medium jar grape jelly

Combine in Crock Pot and cook on low 6 to 8 hours.

CROCKPOT MACARONI AND CHEESE
* 1 (16 oz.) pkg. macaroni, cooked & drained
* 1 tbsp. salad oil
* 1 (13 oz.) can evaporated milk
* 1 1/2 c. milk
* 1 tsp. salt
* 3 c. shredded sharp cheddar cheese
* 1/2 c. melted butter

Lightly grease Crock Pot. Toss macaroni and oil. Add all remaining ingredients.

Stir, cover and cook on low 3 to 4 hours, stirring occasionally.

CROCKPOT MEATBALLS
* 2 pounds Hamburger
* 1 cup Breadcrumbs
* 1 each Egg
* Grated Parmesan cheese
* Parsley and oregano
* Onion and garlic powder
* Milk
* 1 can Beer
* 1 bottle Ketchup, regular size

Mix hamburg, breadcrumbs, egg, seasonings and milk together. Make small meatballs.

Mix ketchup and beer in the Crock Pot and start to heat. You can put the raw meatballs into the sauce and simmer for several hours.

I like to bake the meatballs first to get out most of the grease.

CROCKPOT POTATO SOUP
6-8 potatoes, chunked
2 med. carrots, cubed
2 stalks celery, cubed
1 med. onion, chopped
1 tbsp. parsley flakes
5 c. water
Salt and pepper to taste
Cook in crock pot on low for 8 hours or until vegetables are done. One hour before serving, add one can of evaporated milk.

CROCKPOT ROAST
2 1/2 lb. Chuck roast
2 packets dry Italian dressing mix OR Ranch dressing mix
1 cup water
Place beef in CP, sprinkle seasonings over meat, pour water over all. Cook on low 6-8 hours or until meat shreds easily.

CROCKPOT SCRABBLE
* 2 cups wheat chex
* 2 cups corn chex
* 2 cups rice chex
* 3 cups thin pretzel sticks
* 1 13 ounce can or jar of salted peanuts or asst. mixed nuts
* 1 teaspoon garlic salt
* 1 teaspoon celery salt
* 1/2 teaspoon seasoned salt
* 2 tablespoons grated parmesan cheese
* 1/3 cup melted butter
* 1/3 cup worcestershire sauce
1. In large (double) paper bag, mix together pretzels, cereals, and nuts along with
the garlic salt, celery salt, seasoned salt, and grated cheese.
2. Empty bag into large mixing bowl and sprinkle the melted butter and worcestershire sauce over all mixing gently with your hands.

3. Empty bowl into slow cooker/Crock Pot and cook on low for 3 or 4 hours.

4. Tear open paper bags you used to originally mix the scrabble and spread them out onto a counter.

5. Spread heated slow cooker/Crock Pot scrabble onto torn open bags and let dry for

a minimum of one hour letting the paper absorb any excess moisture.

6. Store in Rubbermaid or Tupperware type airtight containers. Keeps for several weeks without going stale.

CROCKPOT SPAGHETTI SAUCE

4 tbsp. cooking oil
1 sm. onion, finely chopped
1 (15 1/2 oz.) can tomato sauce
1 1/2 c. water
1/2 tsp. pepper
1/2 tsp. red pepper, optional
1 lb. ground beef
1 (29 oz.) can tomato puree
1 (6 oz.) can tomato paste
1 tsp. salt
1/2 tsp. oregano
2 lbs. sausage (Italian links or country style)

Brown ground beef in 2 tablespoon hot oil in frying pan. When almost browned, add onion and continue browning until onion is tender. Pour meat and onion into 3 ½ quart crockpot. Add puree, sauce, paste, water, salt, pepper and oregano and set dial on low setting. Cut 2 lbs. sausage into pieces and brown in remaining 2 tablespoons oil. When brown, place sausages in sauce in crockpot. Continue cooking for 12 hours. (If you like your sauce sweeter, you could add 1/4 to 1/2 cup sugar to this.)

CROCKPOT SPICY DIP

* 2 lb. Velveeta cheese
* 2 lb. hamburger, cooked and drained
* 1 lg. jar Old El Paso taco sauce (or Rotel tomatoes)
* 1 lg. onion, chopped fine

Mix all together in Crock Pot where cheese will melt and all will remaining warm.

CROCKPOT SPLIT PEA SOUP

1 (16 oz.) pkg. dried green split peas, rinsed
1 hambone, or 2 meaty hamhocks, or 2 c. diced ham
3 carrots, peeled & sliced
1 med. onion, chopped
2 stalks of celery plus leaves, chopped
1 or 2 cloves of garlic, minced
1 bay leaf
1/4 c. fresh parsley, chopped (optional)
1 tbsp. seasoned salt (or to taste)
1/2 tsp. fresh pepper
1 1/2 qts. hot water

Layer ingredients in slow cooker, pour in water. DO NOT STIR. Cover and cook on high 4 to 5 hours or on low 8 to 10 hours until peas are very soft and ham falls off bone. Remove bones and bay leaf. Serve garnished with croutons. *Freezes well.

CROCKPOT SWISS STEAK

1 1/2 - 2 lb. round steak
2 tbsp. flour
1 sliced green pepper
1 tsp. salt
1/8 tsp. pepper
2 tbsp. salad oil
1 lg. onion, sliced
1 (16 oz.) can tomatoes, cut up
1 stalk celery, thinly sliced
1 tbsp. thick bottled steak sauce

Cut steak into serving size pieces. Coat with flour, salt and pepper. In large skillet or slow cooking pot with browning unit, brown meat in oil. Pour off excessive fat. In slow cooking pot, combine meat with tomatoes, onion, green pepper and steak sauce. Cover pot and cook on low for 6 to 8 hours or until tender. Thicken juices with additional flour, dissolved in a small amount of water, if desired. Makes 5 or 6 servings. Serve with mashed potatoes.

CROCKPOT TENDERLOIN TIPS

1 lb. tenderloin tips
1 can mushroom soup
1 pkg. onion soup mix
1/4 c. water

Combine ingredients in crock pot. Cook 8 hours. Serve over noodles.

CROCKPOT TURKEY MEATBALLS

* 1 1/2 cups barbecue sauce (your favorite)
* 10 ounces Apple jelly
* 2 tablespoons Tapioca (for thick sauce if desired)
* 1 tablespoon Vinegar
* 1 Egg, beaten
* 1/4 cup Seasoned bread crumbs, fine
* 2 tablespoons Milk
* 1/4 teaspoon Garlic powder
* 1/4 teaspoon salt
* 1/4 teaspoon onion powder
* 1 pound Ground turkey
* Non-stick vegetable spray

In 3 1/2 or 4 quart crockery cooker: stir together barbecue sauce, jelly, tapioca (if used), and vinegar. Cover; cook on high-heat setting while preparing meatballs.

For meatballs, in large bowl combine egg, bread crumbs, milk, garlic powder, salt, and onion powder. Add ground turkey and mix well. Shape into 1/2 to 3/4-inch meatballs. Spray a 12-inch non-stick skillet; add meatballs and brown on all sides over med. heat. Drain meatballs. Add meatballs to crock pot; stir gently. Cover; cook on high heat setting for 1 1/2 to 2 hours. Makes 30 meatballs. Note: for 5 or

6-quart Crock Pot, double all ingredients. Prepare as above. Makes 60 meatballs.

CROCKPOT TURKEY SANDWICHES

6 c. diced turkey
3 c. diced cheese (American or Velveeta)

1 can cream of mushroom soup
1 can cream of chicken soup
1 onion, chopped
1/2 c. Miracle Whip
Mix all of above and put in Crock Pot for 3-4 hours. Stir occasionally. Add liquid, if needed. Serve with buns.

CURRIED FRUIT BAKE

1 package Prunes, (16 oz) pitted
1 package Dried apricots (11 oz)
2 cans Pineapple chunks (13 1/2 oz)
drained
1 can Peaches; sliced (1 lb 13 oz)
1 cup Brown sugar
1/2 teaspoon Curry powder
14 ounces Ginger ale
Combine all ingredients in removable liner. Place in base. Cover and cook on low 4-5 hours or auto 3 hours.

DUMPLING SOUP

* 1 lb. lean steak, cut into 1" cubes
* 1 pkg. onion soup mix
* 6 c. water (hot)
* 2 carrots, peeled & shredded
* 1 stalk finely chopped celery
* 1 tomato, peeled & chopped
* 1 c. pkg. biscuit mix
* 6 tbsp. milk
* 1 tbsp. finely chopped parsley

With pot on low, sprinkle steak with dry onion soup mix. Pour hot water over steak.

Stir in carrots, celery and tomato. Cover and cook on low 4-6 hours or until meat is tender. Turn pot control to HIGH. In separate small bowl, combine biscuit mix with parsley. Stir in milk with fork until mixture is moistened. Drop dumpling mixture into Crock Pot with a teaspoon. Cover and cook on high for about 30 minutes.

5-6 servings.

EASY CHOCOLATE CLUSTERS
* 2 pounds white candy coating , broken into small pieces
* 2 cups semisweet chocolate chips
* 1 pkg.(4 oz) German sweet chocolate
* 1 jar (24 oz) dry roasted peanuts

In a slow cooker, combine candy coating, German chocolate and chocolate chips.

Cover and cook on high for 1 hour, then reduce heat to low. Cover and cook 1 hour longer or until melted, stirring every 15 minutes. Add peanuts and mix well. Drop by teaspoonfuls onto waxed paper; let stand until set. Store at room temperature.

Makes about 3 1/2 dozen.

EGGPLANT PARMIGIANA
* 4 large Eggplant
* 2 Eggs
* 1/3 cup Water
* 3 tablespoons Flour
* 1/3 cup Seasoned bread crumbs
* 1/2 cup Parmesan cheese
* 1 can Marinara sauce, 2 lb
* 1 pound Mozzarella cheese, sliced
* Olive oil, extra virgin

Pare eggplant and cut in 1/2 inch slices; place in bowl in layers and sprinkle each layer with salt and let stand 30 minutes to drain excess water; dry on paper towels. Mix egg with water and flour. Dip eggplant slices in mixture, drain slightly. Saute a few slices at a time quickly in hot olive oil. Combine seasoned bread crumbs with the Parmesan cheese. In removable liner, layer one-fourth of the eggplant, top with one-fourth of the crumbs, one-fourth of the marinara sauce and one-fourth of the mozzarella cheese. Repeat three times to make four layers of eggplant, crumbs, sauce and mozzarella cheese. Place liner in base. Cover and cook on low 4-5 hours or auto 3 hours.

FAVORITE CROCKPOT CHILI

2 lbs. coarsely ground beef chuck
2 (16 oz.) cans red kidney beans, drained
2 (14 1/2 oz.) cans tomatoes, drained
2 med. onions, coarsely chopped
1 green pepper, seeded and coarsely chopped
2 cloves garlic, peel and crushed
2-3 tbsp. chili powder
1 tsp. black pepper
1 tsp. cumin
Salt and pepper to taste

In a large, preferably non-stick, saucepan brown the chuck and drain off the fat. Put the ground beef and other ingredients in a 3 1/2 to 4 quart Crock Pot. If you have a small Crock Pot, cut the recipe in half. Stir well. Cover and cook on low for 10-12 hours. Makes 12 cups of chili

FIESTA CHICKEN
* 2 tablespoons oil
* 3 pounds boneless, skinless chicken breasts, cut into 1-inch pieces
* 1 medium onion, chopped
* 1 teaspoon oregano
* 1 small jalapeno pepper, finely chopped
* 3 cloves garlic, minced
* 1 can (14 1/2 ounce) Mexican style diced tomatoes
* 1/4 teaspoon ground cumin

Heat oil in skillet. Cook chicken pieces until browned. Remove and drain. Place onion, green bell pepper, garlic and jalapeno pepper in skillet and saute until slightly cooked. Add all ingredients to crockpot and stir to combine. Cover; cook on LOW 8 hours (HIGH 4 hours). Serve on flour tortillas.

FRANKS IN SPICY TOMATO SAUCE
* 1 cup ketchup
* 1/2 cup firmly packed brown sugar
* 1 tablespoon red wine vinegar
* 2 teaspoons soy sauce
* 1 teaspoon Dijon mustard
* 1 clove garlic, minced

* 1 pound beef or chicken frankfurters, cut into 1" pieces

Place ketchup, brown sugar, vinegar, soy sauce, mustard, and garlic in the crockery pot. Cover and cook on High until blended. Stir occasionally. Add frankfurters and stir to coat. Cook until thoroughly blended. Serve with toothpicks or wooden skewers to spear franks.

FRESH APPLE COFFEECAKE

2 cups biscuit mix
2/3 cup applesauce
1/4 cup milk
2 tablespoons sugar
2 tablespoons butter or margarine, softened or melted
2 apples, peeled, cored and diced
1 teaspoon cinnamon
1 teaspoon vanilla
1 egg egg, lightly beaten
Streusel
1/4 cup biscuit mix
1/4 cup brown sugar
2 tablespoons firm butter or margarine
1 teaspoon cinnamon
1/4 cup chopped nuts, if desired

Combine first 9 ingredients. Spread in a lightly greased 3 1/2 quart Crock Pot (or spread in a lightly greased baking dish which fits in a larger sized Crock Pot). Combine streusel ingredients with a fork or pastry blender; sprinkle over the batter. Cover and cook on high for about 2 1/2 hours, until a toothpick inserted in the center comes out clean. Uncover and let cool in the pot. When cool enough to handle, loosen the sides and lift out carefully with a flexible spatula, or loosen sides and invert the pot slightly and remove with your hand (you could hold a small piece of foil or waxed paper).

FRIED APPLES

Use these apples as a topping, a filling, or alone topped with whipped cream.

* 3 pounds Granny Smith apples, peeled, cored, and sliced
* 1 teaspoon cinnamon
* dash of fresh grated nutmeg, optional

* 3 tablespoons cornstarch
* 1 cup granulated sugar
* 1 to 2 tablespoons of butter, cut in small pieces

Place apple slices in the slow cooker/Crock Pot; stir in remaining ingredients and dot with the butter. Cover and cook on low for about 6 hours, or until apples are tender but not mushy. Stir about halfway through cooking.

Makes 2 1/2 to 3 cups.

GARLIC CHICKEN WITH CABBAGE

1 whole chicken
1/2-to 1whole red or white onion chopped
3-8 garlic cloves or use garlic salt/powder to your liking
salt and pepper to taste

Season chicken and place in slow cooker/Crock Pot. Add onion and garlice cloves and salt and pepper. Fill slow cooker/Crock Pot 1/4-way with water, cover and cook on high 6-8 hours. The chicken should fall off of the bone.

During the last hour of cooking the chicken, cut up 1 head of green cabbage...I use red also...core removed. Place in a large pot of pan with a shallow amount of water...1/2-to 1-cup. Add two tablespoons of butter or margarine and sprinkle liberally with garlic salt and pepper. Cover and cook on med-high heat for 20-30 minutes. Once chicken and cabbage are done, place some cabbage in a bowl and top with chicken and some of the chicken broth. Talk about yummy. You can alter any of the seasonings and the butter or margarine to your satisfaction.

GARLIC PEPPER CHICKEN PARMESAN

4 chicken leg quarters
2 Tbsp. Mrs. Dash's Gallant Garlics Roasted Garlic Pepper seasoning
1 can Del Monte Zucchini with Tomato Sauce
3 oz. shredded mozzarella cheese

Put chicken in pot. Sprinkle with seasoning. Pour zucchini with tomato sauce over chicken. Cook for 6 hours on high. Sprinkle with cheese and cook until cheese melts - about 30 mins.

GARLIC ROASTED CHICKEN

5 pound Roasting chicken
Salt
Pepper
Paprika
5 Garlic cloves, minced
1/4 pound Sweet butter
1/2 cup Chicken broth

Sprinkle the chicken, inside and out, with salt, pepper and paprika. Spread half of the garlic in the
cavity and spread the rest on the outside of the bird. Place the bird in the slow cooker/Crock Pot and place a few pats of butter on its breast. Add the remaining ingredients and cook on low for 6 to 8 hours. Serve the garlic butter sauce with the chicken.

GERMAN POTATO SALAD

* 2 potatoes, sliced
* 1/2 c. onions, chopped
* 1/2 c. celery sliced
* 1/4 c. green peppers, diced
* 1/4 c. vinegar
* 1/4 c. oil
* Chopped parsley
* Sliced bacon, cooked and crumbled

Combine all ingredients except parsley and bacon. Add salt and pepper to taste.
Stir and cook for 5-6 hours in Crock Pot. Add sugar if needed. Garnish with bacon and parsley.

GINGER BROWN BREAD

* 1 (14-oz.) pkg. gingerbread mix
* 1/4 cup yellow corn meal
* 1 tsp. salt
* 1-1/2 cups milk
* 1/2 cup raisins

Combine gingerbread mix with corn meal and salt in large bowl; stir in milk until mixture is evenly moist. Beat at medium speed with electric mixer for 2 min. Stir in raisins. Pour into a greased and floured 7 or 7 cup mold. Cover with foil and tie. Put a trivet or metal rack in Crock Pot. Pour 2 cups hot water in the pot. Place the filled mold on the rack or the trivet. Cover the pot and cook on high for 3 - 4 hours or until the bread is done. Remove from pot and cool on a rack for 5 min. Loosen the edges with a knife and turn out on a rack and cool slightly. Serve warm with butter or cream cheese.

GLAZED COCKTAIL SAUSAGES
* 3/4 cup apricot preserves
* 1/4 cup prepared yellow mustard
* 2 scallions chopped
* 1/2 pound precooked mini smoked sausages (the ones with cheese in them will work
also)

In a 1-quart mini electric slow cooker; mix together the pre-serves and mustard.

Stir in scallions and sausages. Cover, plug in the cooker and cook for 3 hours or until very hot. Remove the cover, stir to mix and serve immediately with toothpicks; keep the heat on for another 30-60 minutes if desired while serving.

GRAPE JELLY MEATBALLS
* 1 1/2 cups chili sauce
* 1 cup grape jelly (can use currant jelly)
* 1 to 3 teaspoons Dijon mustard
* 1 pound lean ground beef
* 1 egg, lightly beaten
* 3 tablespoons fine dry bread crumbs
* 1/2 teaspoon salt

Combine chili sauce, jelly, and mustard in Crock Pot and stir well. Cook, covered, on high while preparing meatballs.

Combine remaining ingredients and mix thoroughly. Shape in-to 30 meatballs. Bake meatballs in a preheated 400 degree oven for 15 to 20 minutes; drain well. Add meatballs to sauce, stir to coat, cover and cook on low for 6 to 10 hours.

GREEK CHICKEN
6 skinless chicken breasts

1 lg. can tomato sauce
1 sm. can tomato puree
1 can sliced mushrooms
1 can ripe olives
1 tbsp. garlic
1 tbsp. lemon juice
1 tsp. oregano
1 onion, chopped
1/2 c. wine or brandy (optional)
2 c. rice
Salt to taste

Wash and remove fat from chicken. Bake in 350 degree oven for about an hour. Meanwhile, combine all other ingredients except rice). Put chicken and sauce in a slow cooker/Crock Pot on low heat and cook for at least 4 hours to blend flavors. Before serving, cook rice according to directions on box. Serve chicken and sauce over rice.
Serves 6.

GREEK STEW

3 pounds of stewing beef
1 1/2 pounds small onions (about 7)
3 cloves garlic, minced
1- 28 oz. can tomatoes
1/2 cup beef stock
1- 5 1/2 oz. can tomato paste
2 TBS red wine vinegar
2 tsp dried oregano
1/2 tsp each salt & pepper
1/2 cup all purpose flour
1/2 cup cold water
1 sweet green pepper, chopped
1/2 cup crumbled feta cheese
2 Tbsp. chopped fresh parsley

Cut beef into 1 inch cubes, trimming off any fat Cut onions into wedges leaving root end intact. Put meat & onions into slow cooker along with garlic & tomatoes. Combine beef stock, vinegar, oregano, salt & pepper and add to slow cooker, stirring gently to blend. Cook on Low for 8-9 hours or High for 6 hours. Add flour & water mixture and chopped green pepper. Cook on high for 15 minutes or until thickened. Serve sprinkled with feta & parsley.

GREEN BEAN AND POTATO CASSEROLE
        * About 6 cups fresh trimmed and cut green beans (about 2 pounds) or 2 16-ounce
        packages frozen cut green beans
        * 4 to 6 medium red-skinned potatoes, sliced about 1/4-inch
        * 1 large onion, sliced
        * 1 teaspoon dried dill weed
        * 1 teaspoon salt
        * 1/2 teaspoon pepper
        * 1 can cream of chicken soup or other cream soup, undiluted, or use about 1 cup of
        homemade seasoned white sauce, velouté or cheese sauce
        * margarine
Spray the crockpot with cooking spray or lightly grease with butter or margarine.

        Layer sliced potatoes, sliced onion and green beans, sprinkling with dill and salt and pepper as you go. Dot with margarine, about 1 tablespoon total, and add about 2 tablespoons of water. Cover and cook on HIGH for 4 hours (LOW, about 8 hours). Stir in soup or sauce; turn to LOW and cook an additional 30 minutes or leave on WARM
        (Smart-Pot) until serving time or up to 4 hours. Serves 6 to 8. Note: Add bits of cooked bacon for extra flavor.

GREEN CHILE-STUFFED CHICKEN BREASTS
        With the cheese mixture in the center, these chicken breasts come out tender and
        moist.
        * 4 boneless, skinned chicken breast halves, pounded thin
        * 3 ounces cream cheese
        * 3/4 cups shredded Cheddar or Monterey Jack cheese
        * 4 ounces green chiles
        * 1/2 teaspoon chili powder
        * salt and pepper to taste
        * 1 can cream of mushroom soup
        * 1/2 cup hot enchilada sauce

Combine cream cheese, shredded cheese, chiles, chili powder and salt and pepper.

Place a generous dollop on each flattened chicken breast, then roll up. Place chicken rolls in the slow cooker/Crock Pot, seam-side down. Top chicken breast rolls with remaining cheese mixture, soup, and enchilada sauce. Cover and cook on LOW for 6 to 7 hours. Serves 4.

HAMBURGER DIP
* 2 pounds lean ground beef
* 1 cup chopped onion
* 2 cloves garlic, minced or 1/4 teaspoon garlic powder
* salt to taste
* 2 cans (8-ounces each) tomato sauce
* 1/2 cup ketchup
* 1 1/2 teaspoons oregano
* 2 teaspoons white granulated sugar
* 2 package (8-ounces each) cream cheese, softened and cut in cubes
* 2/3 cup grated Parmesan cheese
* 1 teaspoon mild chili powder

In skillet, brown ground beef with onion, discard fat. Pour browned meat and onion into Slow Cooker. Add garlic, salt, tomato sauce, ketchup, oregano, sugar, cream cheese, Parmesan cheese and chili powder. Set slow cooker/Crock Pot on LOW until cream cheese has melted and is thoroughly blended, 1 1/2 to 2 hours. Stir, taste and adjust seasoning if desired. Serve with cube French bread or tortilla chips. If spicier dip is desired, use hot chili powder in place of mild chili powder. Finely chopped jalapenos may be added, if desired.

HEALTHY CROCKPOT CHICKEN CREOLE
* 3 lbs. chicken thighs or breasts, skinned
* 1 cup celery, diced
* 1 red bell pepper, sliced
* 1 green bell pepper, sliced
* 1 onion, sliced
* 1 can sliced mushrooms
* 1 can tomatoes
* 1 tsp. garlic powder

* 3 pkg. sugar substitute
* 1 tsp. Cajun seasoning
* 1/2 tsp. paprika
* salt & pepper to taste
* Louisiana hot sauce to taste
* 2 cups minute rice, cooked

Place chicken in bottom of slow cooker/Crock Pot. Combine remaining ingredients (except rice) & add to slow cooker/Crock Pot. Cook on high 4 to 5 hours or on low 7-8 hours. Cook rice according to package direction. Spoon Creole mixture over hot cooked rice.

HEARTY BEEF DIP

* 8 ounces Cream cheese, cubed
* 1 1/4 ounces Sliced dried beef, diced
* 2 tablespoons Green onion, chopped
* 1/4 cup Milk
* 1/4 cup Pecans, chopped
* 1 Garlic clove

Combine cream cheese and milk in greased Crock Pot. Cover and heat until cheese is melted, 30 to 60 minutes. Add remaining ingredients; stir thoroughly. Cover and heat 30 minutes.

Serve with crackers or bread pieces.

HEARTY CHILI

1 pound ground turkey
1/2 ground chuck
30 oz. tomato sauce
24 oz. V-8 (tomato-vegetable juice)
1/2 c. chopped onion
1/2 c. chopped celery
1 tbsp. chili powder
1 c. chopped green pepper
1 c. chopped mushrooms
1 sm. jalapeno pepper (optional)
14 oz. stewed tomatoes
1/2 c. uncooked wild rice
2/3 c. brown sugar

14 oz. chili beans

1 oz. chili seasoning mix

Brown ground turkey and ground beef. Drain well. Place all other ingredients in a slow cooker and add the meat. Cook on low for 6 to 9 hours. Serve with crackers or cornbread.

HOME-STYLE BREAD PUDDING

2 Eggs, slightly beaten

2 1/4 cups Milk

1 teaspoon Vanilla

1/2 teaspoon Cinnamon

1/4 teaspoon Salt

2 cups 1-inch bread cubes

1/2 cup Brown sugar

1/2 cup Raisins or chopped dates

In medium mixing bowl, combine eggs with milk, vanilla, cinnamon, salt, bread, sugar, and raisins

or dates. Pour into 1 1/2-quart baking or souffle dish. Place metal trivet (or aluminum foil shaped

in a ring to keep the dish off the bottom of the pot) or rack in bottom of slow cooker/Crock Pot.

Add 1/2 cup hot water. Set baking dish on trivet. Cover pot; cook on high for about 2 hours. Serve pudding warm or cool.

Makes 4 to 6 servings.

HONEYED CHICKEN WINGS

* 3 lb. chicken wings

* Salt & pepper, to taste

* 1 c. honey

* 1/2 c. soy sauce

* 2 tbsp. vegetable oil

* 2 tbsp. ketchup

* 1/2 garlic clove, minced

Cut off and discard chicken wing tips. Cut each wing into 2 parts and sprinkle with salt and pepper. Combine remaining ingredients and mix well. Place wings in slow cooker and pour sauce over. Cook 6 to 8 hours on low.

HOT ARTICHOKE DIP
* 6 ounces Artichoke hearts, marinated
* 1/3 cup Mayonnaise
* 1 tablespoon Pimento, diced (optional)
* 1/2 cup Parmesan cheese, grated
* 1/3 cup Sour cream
* 1/8 teaspoon Garlic powder

Drain and chop artichoke hearts. Combine all ingredients and place in Crock Pot. Cover and heat 30 to 60 minutes until hot. Serve with tortilla chips or assorted crackers.

HOT BROCCOLI DIP
* 1 (10 oz.) chopped frozen broccoli, thawed
* 1 stick margarine
* 1 med. onion, chopped
* 1 (10 3/4 oz.) cans of cream of mushroom soup
* 14 oz. Velveeta cheese, cut up
* 1 to 2 1/2 oz. can mushroom stems and pieces

Combine first 3 ingredients in a saute pan and cook until onions are clear. Transfer to the slow cooker/Crock Pot. Add soup, cheese, and mushrooms, heat on low for about 1 1/2 to 2 hours, or until cheese is melted and mixture is hot. Dip with large corn chips or can be poured over baked potatoes. Freezes well.

HOT CARAMEL APPLES
4 Lg. tart apples, cored
1/2 C. apple juice
8 Tblspoons brown sugar
12 red-hot candies
4 Tblspoons butter or margarine
8 caramels
1/4 tsp. ground cinnamon

Peel about 3/4 inch off the top of each apple; place in crock. Pour juice over apples. Fill the center of each apple with 2 Tblspoons of sugar, 3 red-hots, 1Tblspoon of butter and 2 caramels. Sprinkle with cinnamon. Cover and cook on low for 4-6 hours or until apples are tender. May serve immediately with whipped cream if desired.

Makes 4 servings.

HOT CHICKEN SANDWICHES
12 eggs
1 loaf of bread (cubed)
2 large (or 3 small) boiler chickens (reserve some broth for use in
recipe)
salt to taste
pepper to taste
Boil the chickens until done and let cool. When the chicken meat is completely cool to the touch, pick the chicken meat from the bones and set aside. Reserve a little of the broth for later.

Cube the loaf of bread and put it in a large bowl. Mix in the 12 eggs with the cubed bread. Add the chicken meat you picked from the bone and enough broth from the chicken to moisten. Add salt and pepper to your own taste. Mix well. Spread mixture into a lightly greased casserole dish and bake in a preheated 350 degrees F (175 degrees C) oven for 30 minutes. Or spray a slow cooker/Crock Pot with cooking spray to prevent sticking and pour in the chicken mixture. Let cook on low for about 6 hours. Serve by scooping onto buns.

Makes 12 to 18 servings

Tina's Comments: My husband thinks it could use some chopped up onions in it (I'm not an onion fan......) but I did add a little bit of parsley to it.

HOT CHILI CON QUESO
* 1 1/2 cups half-and-half, scalded
* 1/2 pound grated Monterrey Jack cheese
* 1/2 pound grated sharp process cheese
* 1 tablespoon butter
* 1/2 onion, minced
* 1 medium clove garlic, minced
* 1/4 cup dry white wine or low-sodium stock
* 1/4 cup flour
* 1/4 cup water
* 1 can chopped green chile peppers (4 oz)
* 1 to 2 tablespoons chopped jalapeno (more or less depending on taste)

* salt and pepper
* dash cayenne pepper

Pour scalded half-and-half into buttered Crock Pot. Turn to high and stir in
cheeses.

In small skillet, saute onion and garlic in butter until onion is tender. Add wine or stock and stir well. Add to cheese mixture. Combine flour with water and stir in. Cook covered on high for 30 minutes, or until cheese begins to melt. Turn to low and cook about 4 to 6 hours, stirring 2 or 3 times during the first hour and occasionally after that. If the mixture is too thin, mix 2 tablespoons of flour with 2 tablespoons of water and add. Serve warm with tortilla chips and/or other dippers.

HOT DOG AND BACON ROLLUPS
* 2 pkg. hot dogs, cut in half
* brown sugar
* 1 lb. bacon, cut into in the middle

Take a piece of hot dog and piece of bacon, wrap bacon around hot dog. Stick a toothpick through bacon to hold. Place one layer in bottom of Crock Pot and cover with brown sugar. Repeat until all the hot dogs have been used. Cook 3 to 4 hours.

HOT DOG HORS D'OEUVRES
* 2 (1 lb.) pkgs all beef hot dogs, sliced in half
* 1 lb. bacon, sliced in half
* Brown sugar

Wrap each hot dog half with bacon strip. Fasten with toothpick. Layer in slow cooker/Crock Pot, sprinkling each layer with a thin layer of brown sugar. Repeat layers until hot dogs run out. Cook on low for 2-3 hours, stirring gently with wooden spoon every 30 minutes.

HOT FRUIT COMPOTE
1 can peaches, drained
1 can pears, drained
1 can pineapple chunks, drained

1 cup brown sugar
1 tsp. cinnamon
1/2 stick margarine (4oz)
1 can cherry pie filling
Cut all fruit into bite-size pieces. Add rest of ingredients. Stir all together. Cover and cook on low 3 to 6 hours. Use as a side dish for breakfast or a meal, or as a topping for a dessert.

HOT 'N' SPICY PECANS
* 1/4 cup butter, cut in pieces (4 oz)
* 6 cups pecans
* 2 teaspoons chili powder
* 1/2 teaspoon onion salt
* 1/2 teaspoon garlic powder

Place cut up butter in Crock Pot and heat, uncovered, on high until melted (15 to 20 minutes). Add pecans; stir to coat.

Cover and cook on high 30 minutes. Uncover and cook on high 2 1/2 hours longer, stirring occasionally.

Sprinkle with the seasonings and toss to coat; Spread on a baking sheet to cool.

Store in an airtight container in the refrigerator for up to 6 weeks, or freeze for up to 3 months. Serve at room temperature or warm.

HOT SPINACH DIP
* 2 (10 oz.) pkgs. frozen chopped spinach
* 1 lg. jar jalapeno Cheez Whiz
* 1 can cream of mushroom soup
* 1 (3 oz.) pkg. cream cheese
* 2 tbsp. dried minced onion

Thaw spinach completely. Drain, and squeeze as much moisture as possible from spinach. Combine all ingredients in the slow cooker/Crock Pot and cook on low about 2 hours, until hot (stir a few times to blend well). Keep warm in Crock Pot or chafing dish. Serve with corn chips or crackers.

INDIAN PUDDING
* 3 c. milk
* 1/2 c. cornmeal

* 1/2 tsp. salt
* 3 eggs
* 1/4 c. light brown sugar
* 1/3 c. molasses
* 2 tbsp. butter
* 1/2 tsp. cinnamon
* 1/4 tsp. allspice
* 1/2 tsp. ginger

Lightly grease crockpot. Preheat on high for 20 minutes. Meanwhile bring milk, cornmeal and salt to a boil. Boil, stirring constantly, for 5 minutes. Cover and simmer an additional 10 minutes. In a large bowl, combine remaining ingredients. Gradually beat in hot cornmeal mixture and whisk until smooth. Pour into crock and cook on high for 2 to 3 hours or low for 6 to 8 hours.

INSTANT APPETIZER MEATBALLS

I find the following to be a real crowd pleaser: I take about half a bag of those great frozen meatballs from Sam's Club and dump them into the slow cooker/Crock Pot. Then I take 2 packages of brown gravy, mix them up according to the directions and then pour over the meatballs. Heat on low for 4 hours or so and you have instant appetizers.

ITALIAN GREEN BEANS

1/3-1/2 lb. sweet Italian sausage
15 oz can stewed tomatoes, chopped
4 cans(8 oz) sliced mushrooms (do not drain)
1/4-1/2 tsp. onion &/or garlic powders
1/2 tsp. basil &/or oregano
3 (1 lb.) cans Italian style green beans, 2 of them drained
1/2 cup Parmesan cheese

Brown sausage and drain. Add all ingredients except green beans. Mix thoroughly and simmer for 15 minutes. Add green beans and mix. Bake at 250 degrees in a covered casserole for 30 minutes to 2 hours; or in a slow cooker on low up to 3 hours.

JERK CHICKEN

(A traditional Jamaican dish adapted to the crockpot)
1 large onion, cut into 8 pieces

1 generous tablespoon chopped crystallized ginger
1/2 to 1 habanero pepper, seeded, deveined, and finely minced (wear
gloves!)
1/2 teaspoon ground allspice
2 tablespoons dry mustard
1 teaspoon freshly ground black pepper
2 tablespoons red wine or balsamic vinegar
2 tablespoons soy sauce
2 cloves garlic, crushed and minced
3 to 4 pounds chicken tenders

Combine onion and ginger in a food processor; process until finely chopped. Add remaining ingredients, except chicken, and pulse until well combined. Place chicken in a 3 1/2-quart (or larger) slow cooker/Crock Pot and cover with sauce. Cover, set on low, and cook for 6 to 8 hours. or until chicken is tender (3 to 4 hours on high).

4 servings.

LAZY CROCKPOT CHICKEN

1 pkg. boneless chicken breasts
1 can cream of mushroom soup
1/4 c. flour
1 jar sliced mushrooms
Salt, pepper and paprika

Rinse chicken breasts. Put salt, pepper and paprika on both sides. Place in Crock Pot. Mix other ingredients together. Add to Crock Pot. Cook on LOW all day. Serve over noodles, rice, or mashed potatoes.

LEMON BAKED CHICKEN

16 ounces skinned and boned uncooked chicken breasts, cut into 4 pieces
1 lemon
1 teaspoon lemon pepper
1 teaspoon paprika

Place chicken pieces in a slow cooker. Squeeze juice of half a lemon over chicken. Sprinkle lemon pepper and paprika over top. Cut remaining lemon half into thin slices. Arrange slices around chicken. Cover and cook on HIGH for 4 hours.

LEMON-GARLIC CHICKEN
3 pounds Chicken
1/2 cup Lemon juice
1/2 cup Garlic cloves, crushed
1 teaspoon Seasoned salt
1 teaspoon Poultry seasoning
2 dashes Tabasco
1 cup White wine

Skin and cut up chicken. Combine with other ingredients in slow cooker/Crock Pot. Set on low.

Upon return from work, debone chicken. Serve over rice. If you freeze chicken pieces separately, and mix up other ingredients the night before, you can dump it all together quickly in the morning. And if you start with frozen chicken it doesn't fall apart.

LEMON PEPPER CHICKEN
5 boneless skinless chicken breasts (or any chicken pieces)
Lemon Pepper seasoning
2 tbsp. melted or squeeze margarine

Put chicken in slow cooker/Crock Pot. Sprinkle generously with seasoning. Pour margarine over chicken. Cook on low for 10 hrs. or on high for 6 hrs.

LEMON-POPPYSEED UPSIDE DOWN CAKE
This cake makes its own custard-like topping.
1 pkg. Lemon-Poppyseed Bread Mix
1 egg
8 ounces light sour cream
1/2 cup water
Sauce:
1 tablespoon butter
3/4 cup water
1/2 cup sugar
juice from one lemon (about 1/4 cup)

Mix the first 4 ingredients together until well moistened. Spread batter in a lightly greased 3 ½ quart slow cooker/Crock Pot. Combine sauce ingredients in a small saucepan; bring to a boil. Pour boiling mixture over the batter; cover and cook on high for 2 to 2 1/2 hours. Edges will be slightly browned. Turn heat off and leave in the pot for about 30 minutes with cover slightly ajar. When cool enough to handle, hold a large plate over the top of the pot then invert.

LEMON-ROSEMARY CHICKEN

1/2 c. lemon juice
1 tbsp. vegetable oil
1 garlic clove, crushed
1 teaspoon. dried rosemary
1/4 teaspoon. salt
1/4 teaspoon. pepper
1 1/2 to 2 lbs.boneless, skinless chicken breasts

In a large food storage bag, place lemon juice, oil, garlic, rosemary, salt and pepper. Add chicken.

Close bag and marinate in refrigerator 4 hours or overnight, turning bag frequently. Place chicken in the slow cooker/Crock Pot and pour marinade over. Cover and cook for 6 to 8 hours, or until tender, basting occasionally with the marinade, if possible. You may add frozen broccoli and carrots about 1 to 1 1/2 hours before done.

Serves 4 to 6.

LEMON TARRAGON CHICKEN WITH ASPARAGUS

1 pound frozen chicken breasts, boneless
1/4 cup lemon juice
1/4 cup chicken stock
1 teaspoon tarragon (dried)
1 package frozen asparagus (or fresh partially cooked)
2 tablespoons flour
1/2 cup heavy or whipping cream
salt and pepper to taste

Put frozen chicken breasts in Crock Pot and add lemon juice, broth, and tarragon. Cook on low 6 hours. Add asparagus; whisk cream and flour together and add. Cook another hour on high or until asparagus is tender and sauce is thickened. Serve over noodles or rice. Artichokes are good in this too!

Lo-Cal Crock Pot Chicken
   2 med. onions, thinly sliced
   2-3 lb. chicken, cut up and skinned
   2 cloves garlic, minced
   1 lg. can tomatoes
   1 tsp. salt
   1/4 tsp. pepper
   1/2 tsp. oregano, crushed
   1/2 tsp. basil
   1/2 tsp. celery seed
   1 bay leaf
   Layer in order and cook on low 6-8 hours, or on high 2 1/2 - 4 hours.

LOW-FAT CHICKEN & VEGGIE BAKE
   8 boneless, skinless chicken breasts
   2 cans whole potatoes, drained
   1 tsp garlic powder
   1 bottle fat free Italian salad dressing
   1 pkg frozen veggies
   1 can water chestnuts (optional)
   salt & pepper
   Sprinke chicken breasts with salt, pepper and garlic. Put chicken in bottom of slow cooker/Crock Pot. Add remaining ingredients. Cook on high for 4-6 hours or on low for 8-10 hours.
   Serves 8

LOW-FAT GLAZED CHICKEN IN SLOW COOKER
   6 ounces orange juice, frozen concentrate-thawed
   3 chicken breasts, split
   1/2 tsp marjoram
   1 dash ground nutmeg
   1 dash garlic powder (optional)

1/4 cup water

2 Tbsp cornstarch

Combine thawed orange juice concentrate (not regular orange juice) in bowl along with the marjoram, garlic powder and nutmeg. Split the chicken breasts to make 6 serving sizes. Dip pieces into the orange juice to coat completely. Place in slow cooker/Crock Pot. Pour the remaining orange juice mixture over the chicken. Cover and cook on low for 7-9 hours, or cook on high for 4 hours if you wish. Precise cooking time is not important in slow cooker/Crock Pot cooking. When chicken is done, remove to serving platter. Pour the sauce that remains into a saucepan. Mix the cornstarch and water and stir into the juice in pan. Cook over medium heat, stirring constantly, until thick and bubbly. Serve the sauce over the chicken.

LUSCIOUS LEMON CHEESECAKE

Crust:

1 cup vanilla wafer crumbs

1/2 teaspoon lemon zest

1 tablespoons sugar

3 tablespoons butter, melted

Filling:

16 ounces cream cheese

2/3 cup sugar

2 large eggs

1 tablespoon flour or cornstarch

1 teaspoon fresh lemon zest

2 tablespoons fresh lemon juice

Combine crust ingredients. Pat into a 7-inch springform pan.

Beat cream cheese and sugar together until smooth; beat in eggs and continue beating on medium speed of a hand-held electric mixer for about 3 minutes. Beat in remaining ingredients and continue beating for about 1 minute. Pour batter into the prepared crust. Place the cheesecake on a rack in the Crock Pot. Cover and cook on high for 2 1/2 to 3 hours. Let stand in the covered pot after turning it off for about an hour or 2, until cool enough to handle. Cool thoroughly before removing pan sides. Chill in the refrigerator before serving, and refrigerate any leftovers.

MACARONI PIE
8 oz. box (cooked) macaroni
3 c. grated cheese
1 (16 oz.) can of evaporated milk
1 1/2 c. sweet milk
2 eggs
1/4 c. margarine
1 tsp. sugar
Salt and pepper to taste
Combine cooked macaroni with other ingredients and pour into a greased crockpot.
Cook 3 1/2 hours on medium heat.

MANHATTEN MEATBALLS
* 1 lb ground beef
* 1 lb. mild pork sausage (or use all beef)
* 2 c. soft bread crumbs or 1 1/2 c. oatmeal
* 2 eggs
* 1/2 c. chopped onion
* 2 tbsp. parsley
* 2 tsp. salt
* 1/2 tsp. garlic salt
Sauce:
* 1 (12 oz) jar apricot preserves
* 1/2 c. barbecue sauce
Mix first 8 ingredients together and form meatballs. Brown in skillet, or in oven at 450 degrees for 15 minutes. Heat sauce, pour over meatballs. Bake at 350 degrees for 25 minutes or cook in Crock Pot. Can be served over rice or as an appetizer with toothpicks.
Makes 4 or 5 dozen.

MAPLE-FLAVORED BARBECUE CHICKEN
1 c. ketchup
1/2 c. maple flavored syrup
2 tbsp. prepared mustard
2 tbsp. Worcestershire sauce
2 tsp. lemon juice

1/2 tsp. chili powder
1/4 tsp. garlic powder
4 boneless, skinned chicken breasts
Place all ingredients in slow cooker/Crock Pot and cook on low for about 7 to 8 hours or until chicken is done. Remove meat, shred and return to sauce. Place on buns for sandwiches or serve over hot rice.
Serves 4 to 6.

MAPLE GLAZED SWEET POTATOES

5 medium sweet potatoes
1/4 cup brown sugar
1/4 cup pure maple syrup
1/4 cup apple cider
dash salt and pepper to taste
Peel sweet potatoes and cut into 1/4 to 1/2-inch thick slices; place in Crock Pot. Whisk remaining ingredients together and pour over potatoes. Cover and cook on low 7 to 9 hours. Stir a few times, if possible, to keep them coated.
Serves 4.

MARINER FONDUE

* 2 cans (10 3/4 oz each) condensed cream of celery soup
* 2 c. grated sharp process cheese
* 1 c. chunked cooked lobster
* 1/2 c. chopped cooked shrimp
* 1/2 c. chopped cooked crabmeat
* 1/4 c. finely chopped, cooked scallops
* dash paprika
* dash cayenne peppe
* 1 loaf of French bread, cut into 1 inch cubes
Combine all ingredients except bread cubes in lightly greased Crock-Pot; stir thoroughly. Cover and cook on High for 1 hour or until cheese is melted. Turn to Low for serving. Using fondue forks, dip bread cubes into fondue.
Makes about 1 1/2 qts.

MARMALADE-GLAZED CARROTS
1 package (32oz) fresh baby carrots
1/2 cup marmalade
1 tablespoon water
2 tablespoon brown sugar
1 tablespoon butter
1/2 teaspoon cinnamon
1/4 teaspoon nutmeg
1 tablespoons cornstarch
2 tablespoons water
salt and pepper to taste

Combine all ingredients in Crock Pot and cook on low for 7 to 9 hours, until carrots are tender.

About 15 minutes before serving, make a paste of the cornstarch and cold water; stir into carrots. Taste and adjust seasonings.

Serves 4 to 6 as a side dish.

MEATBALLS
* 2 pounds Ground beef
* 1 medium Onion-grated or minced
* 20 Ritz crackers, crushed
* 1/4 teaspoon Black pepper
* 1/4 teaspoon Garlic salt
* 1/2 teaspoon Dry mustard
* 2 large Eggs, beaten
* 1 1/2 cups Bottled Barbecue Sauce
* 3/4 cup Tomato paste
* 1 teaspoon Liquid smoke
* 1/3 cup Catsup
* 1/3 cup Brown sugar
* 1/2 cup Water or as needed

In a large bowl combine the ground beef, onion, crushed crackers, pepper, garlic salt, dry mustard and eggs. Squish the mixture together by hand until well mixed and form into walnut sized balls. Place them on a flat wire rack in a roasting pan or a large cake pan. Bake the meatballs in a 350 degree oven for 15 minutes, turn and bake for 15 minutes more. In a Crock Pot combine the remaining ingredients.

Cook on high 30 minutes. Add the meatballs and simmer for several hours.

Makes about 60 meatballs.

MEDITERRANEAN STYLE CHICKEN
6 skinless and boneless chicken breasts
1 large can tomato sauce
1 small can tomato puree
1 can sliced mushrooms
1 can ripe olives, sliced or whole
1 tablespoon garlic
1 tablespoon lemon juice
1 teaspoon oregano
1 onion, chopped
1/2 cup wine or brandy (optional)
cooked rice
Salt to taste

Wash and remove excess fat from chicken. Combine all ingredients in the slow cooker/Crock Pot, except the rice. Cover and cook on low for 6 to 8 hours. Serve chicken and sauce over rice.

Serves 6.

MEXICAN CHEESE DIP
* 1/2 pound Velveeta
* 1 teaspoon Taco seasoning (optional)
* 1/2 can Ro-Tel Tomatoes with chilies

Cube cheese and place in Crock Pot. Cover and heat 30 to 60 minutes, until melted, stirring occasionally. Stir in tomatoes and seasoning. Cover and continue heating 30 minutes.

Serve with tortilla chips or corn chips.

MEXICAN CHICKEN IN CROCKPOT
* Chicken pieces
* Taco seasoning

Let cook all day on low or several hours on high. Serve as chicken tacos or with a side dish as the main course. Super simple. You really cannot go wrong. Be careful because if you cook too long the bones could come apart into small pieces and could be difficult to separate from meat.

MEXICAN CHILI
2 (15 1/2 oz.) cans red kidney beans, drained
1 (28 oz.) can tomatoes, cut up
1 c. chopped celery
1 c. chopped onion
1 (6 oz.) can tomato paste
1/2 c. chopped green pepper
1 (4 oz.) can green chili peppers, drained and chopped
2 tbsp. sugar
1 bay leaf
1/2 tsp. garlic powder
1 tsp. salt
1 tsp. dried, crushed marjoram
Dash of pepper
1 lb. ground beef

In skillet brown ground beef and drain. In crockery cooker combine all ingredients. Cover, cook on low heat for 8 to 10 hours. Remove bay leaf and stir before serving. Approximately 10 servings and great with corn bread!

MINT BUTTER WAFERS
* 2 T. butter
* 1/4 C. milk
* 1 pkg. white frosting mix (dry)
* 3 drops peppermint flavoring

Melt butter and milk together in a covered cooker on high. Stir in frosting and cook 1 to 2 minutes more. Add flavoring. Turn to low and drop by teaspoonfuls onto waxed paper.
Makes 5 dozen.

MIXED VEGETABLE BAKE
* 2 cans Creamed corn, 17 oz each
* 2 cans Green beans; cut, 16 oz each

* 2 cans Peas, 16 oz each
* 1 can Tomatoes, 17 oz
* 1/2 cup Mayonnaise
* 1 teaspoon Tarragon
* 1 teaspoon Basil
* 1/2 teaspoon Salt
* Pepper

Combine all ingredients in removable liner, mix well to blend herbs. Place liner in base. Cover and cook on low 4-6 hours.

NO-BEAN CHILI

2 pounds ground beef, or cubed lean stew beef
1 (8 oz) can Tomato sauce
1 (6 oz) can Tomato paste
1 (16 oz) can Stewed tomatoes , optional
2 tablespoons Chili powder
1 1/2 teaspoons Salt
1 teaspoon Hot pepper sauce, or more

Combine all ingredients in slow cooker. Cover and cook on low for 8-10 hours. (Add a can of your favorite beans if you wish.)
Serves 4 to 6.

OLD FASHIONED CROCKPOT APPLE BUTTER

14 cooking apples (Winesap)
2 1/2 c. sugar
1 c. apple juice
1 tbsp. cinnamon
1 tbsp. cloves
1 tsp. Allspice

Wash and core apples; cut in 1/4 pieces. Slightly grease crockpot, put in apples and apple juice. Cook on high for 5 hours. Add other ingredients and cook for 6 hours on high. Stir each hour. Pack in 1/2 pint jars and seal. Makes 5 (1/2 pint) jars.

ONE POT CHICKEN AND GRAVY

Boneless, skinless chicken breasts
Potatoes, quartered, with jackets
About 6 stalks celery

1/2 pkg baby carrots
1 can cream of chicken soup*
1 pkg dry onion soup mix

Place vegetables on bottom of Crock Pot. Brown chicken breasts in PAM or vegetable spray. Place over vegetables. Cover with the cream of chicken soup, undiluted. Sprinkle with dry onion soup mix. Do not add water. Cover and cook all day on low, or 6 hours on high.

    * I had planned to substitute either Campbell's healthy choice or reduced fat cream of chicken. I have done this in other recipes, and cannot taste the difference.

ORANGE-GLAZED CHICKEN
6 ounces orange juice, frozen concentrate, thawed
6 chicken breast halves
1/2 teaspoon marjoram
1 dash ground nutmeg
1 dsah garlic powder
1/4 cup water
2 tablespoons cornstarch

Combine thawed orange juice concentrate in a bowl with the marjoram, garlic powder and nutmeg.

    Dip each chicken breast half into the orange juice to coat completely. Place in slow cooker/Crock Pot. Pour the remaining orange juice mixture over the chicken. Cover and cook on low for 6-8 hours, or on high for about 4 hours.

ORANGE BURGUNDY CHICKEN
* 2 1/2 to 3 pounds frying chicken, cut up
* 1/2 cup orange marmalade
* 1/2 cup orange juice
* 1/2 cup dry red wine
* 2 tablespoons cornstarch
* 2 tablespoons brown sugar, packed
* 1 tablespoon lemon juice
* 1 teaspoon salt

Remove skin from chicken. Rinse and place in slow cooker. Combine remaining ingredients in a bowl and pour over chicken.

Cover and cook on low 6 to 8 hours. Serve with rice and spinach salad.

Serves 6.

ORANGE GLAZED CARROTS (CROCKPOT)

* 3 cups Thinly sliced carrots
* 3 tablespoons Butter or margarine
* 2 cups Water
* 3 tablespoons Orange marmalade
* 1/4 teaspoon Salt
* 2 tablespoons Chopped pecans

Combine carrots, water, and salt in Crock Pot. Cover and cook on high 2 to 3 hours or until the carrots are done. Drain well; stir in remaining ingredients. Cover and cook on high 20-30 minutes.

Makes 5 to 6 servings.

PAPRIKOSH

5 large Carrots (cubed)
8 large Potatoes (cubed)
5 large Celery stalks
2 large Onions (sliced thin)
3 tablespoons Paprika*, salt & pepper to taste

Throw all ingredients into the slow cooker/Crock Pot, add water to top veggies (it makes a sort of "gravy") and cook on high for 4 hours.

PARMESAN SCALLOPED POTATOES

5 to 6 red potatoes, sliced (about 5 cups sliced)
6 slices turkey bacon or other smoked meat
3 ounces freshly grated parmesan cheese
1 can condensed cream of mushroom soup
salt and pepper to taste

Layer all ingredients in lightly buttered 3 1/2-quart Crock Pot (or use a souffle dish to fit in a larger Crock Pot); cover and cook on low for 7 to 9 hours. Adjust seasonings.

Serves 4.

PARTY HAMBURGER DIP

* 1 pound Hamburger

* 1 1/2 pounds Velveeta
* 1 can Ro-Tel tomatoes and chiles
* 1/2 Onion, diced
* 1 8 - 12 oz fresh mushrooms, sliced

Brown hamburger, mushrooms & onion; drain. Melt Velveeta in slow cooker. Add remaining ingredients and simmer (high) for about 30 minutes. Serve with corn chips or crackers. Turn pot to low while serving.

PARTY MIX

* 7 cups assorted cereal (oat, rice, wheat in various shapes)
* 1 cup peanuts, pecans, cashews, or mixed nuts
* 1 cup mini pretzel sticks
* 1/2 cup butter or margarine, melted
* 4 tablespoons Worcestershire sauce
* dash hot pepper sauce
* 1/2 teaspoon seasoned salt
* 1/2 teaspoon garlic salt
* 1/2 teaspoon onion salt

Combine cereals, nuts and pretzels in Crock Pot. Mix melted butter with remaining ingredients and pour over the cereal mixture, tossing to coat. Cook uncovered on high for 2 hours, stirring about every 30 minutes. Turn to low and cook another 2 to 6 hours. Store in an airtight container. Makes about 10 cups.

PASTA AND BROCCOLI

1 med. onion
1 can cream of mushroom soup
1 lb. Velveeta
1 pkg. frozen broccoli & cauliflower
1 pkg. shell noodles

Mix onion, cream of mushroom soup and Velveeta in a slow cooker/Crock Pot on high until melted. Add broccoli and cauliflower until hot. Add cooked shells right before serving.

PEACH BUTTER

6 cups unsweetened peaches
3 cups white sugar
1 1/2 cups apricot nectar

2 tablespoons orange or lemon juice

1 teaspoon vanilla

Put peaches through food mill or food processor. Mix all ingredients together well and put in Crock Pot. Bring to a good boil, uncover and boil until thick or 4 hours, high or low to keep it boiling. When it boils good, remove cover.

PHEASANT AND WILD RICE

1 cup raw wild raw rice

1 can cream of mushroom soup

1 can cream of chicken soup

1 can mushrooms

2 1/2 cups water

2 pheasants, cut up, flour and brown

1 pkg instant onion soup mix

Mix rice, canned soup, water, mushrooms and water together in slow cooker/Crock Pot. Place

pheasants in slow cooker/Crock Pot (I never brown mine, I just put them in and they come out fine). Sprinkle with onion soup mix. Cover. Cook on low 6 to 8 hours. Add a splash more water if rice is looking dry towards end of cooking time.

PHILIPPINE CHICKEN

* 1 chicken, cut up

* 1 cup water

* 1/2 cup vinegar

* 1/4 cup soy sauce

* 2 cloves garlic, sliced

Put all in Crock Pot; cook for 6 to 8 hours on low. Serve over rice.

PICANTE CHEESE DIP

* 1 1/2 pounds ground beef (browned)

* 1 can (11 oz.) cream of mushroom soup

* 2 pound processed cheese (Velveeta)

* 1 stick margarine

* 1 onion, chopped

* 2 tbsp. chili powder

* 1 cup picante sauce

Brown meat and onion. Drain. Add all ingredients to slow cooker/Crock Pot and cook on low heat until cheese melts, about 1 1/2 hours. Serve in slow cooker/Crock Pot with tortilla chips.

PIZZA DIP
* 1 large cream cheese softened
* 1 jar pizza sauce
* 1 small can chopped olives
* 1 medium onion chopped
* 1 pkg. sliced pepperoni
* 1 pkg. grated cheese for pizza

Spread cream cheese in bottom of slow cooker/Crock Pot. Then mix up the pizza sauce, onion, olives and pepperoni and spread on top of the cream cheese. Sprinkle with the pizza cheese and cook on low until the cheese on top melts. Serve with tortilla chips.

You could add other pizza toppings to this or delete some that are listed.

PIZZA FONDUE
* 1 lb. ground beef
* 2 cans Chef Boy-ardee pizza sauce with cheese
* 8 oz. grated cheddar cheese
* 8 oz. grated Mozzarella
* 1 tsp. oregano
* 1/2 tsp. fennel seed
* 1 tbsp. cornstarch

Brown ground beef and drain. Add all other ingredients place in slow cooker/Crock Pot and heat through.

Serve with tortilla chips.

POTATO CASSEROLE
1 pkg frozen hash browns
1 small carton Ranch Dip
1 can Cream of Potato Soup
salt, pepper
dried onions to taste
4-5 oz of grated cheddar cheese

Mix 1st 4 ingredients. Put into slow cooker/Crock Pot. Place grated cheese on top. I cooked on high for about 4 hours. They were delicious. You could probably add ham or other meat, for a complete meal in one.

POTATOES PERFECT
1/4 pound Bacon, diced
2 md Onions, thinly sliced
4 md Potatoes, thinly sliced
1/2 pound Cheddar cheese, thinly slice
Salt and pepper
Butter

Line slow cooker/Crock Pot with aluminum foil, leaving enough to overlap poatoes when finished.

Layer half each of the bacon, onions, potatoes and cheese in slow cooker/Crock Pot. Season to taste and dot with butter. Repeat layers of bacon, onions, potatoes and cheese. Dot with butter. Overlap with remaining foil. Cover and cook on low setting for 10 to 12 hours.

PROVINCIAL CHICKEN
* 1 1/2 pounds chicken tenders, frozen
* 2 small zucchini, diced
* 1 can (4 oz) sliced black olives
* 1 tablespoon sherry wine vinegar or balsamic vinegar
* 1 can good-quality diced tomatoes (about 15 ounces)
* 1 can (10 oz) cream of chicken soup with herbs
* 2 teaspoons dried parsley flakes
* 1 teaspoon dried basil
* 1 tablespoon dried minced onion
* 1 cup shredded cheddar cheese
* 2 to 3 tablespoons sour cream (optional)
* hot noodles, rice or pasta

Combine first 9 ingredients in 3 1/2-quart slow cooker/Crock Pot (or larger). Cover and cook on low for 6 to 8 hours. Add cheese and sour cream during the last 15 minutes. Serve over hot noodles, rice or pasta.

PUDDING CAKE

1 cup Flour
1/2 cup Sugar
1/2 cup Coarsely chopped pecans, or walnuts
1/4 cup Unsweetened cocoa
2 teaspoons Baking powder
1/2 teaspoon Salt
1/2 cup Milk
1/4 cup Oil
1 teaspoon Vanilla extract
1 cup Boiling water
1/2 cup Chocolate syrup
Whipped cream or ice cream

Mix together first 6 ingredients in 6-cup mold. Stir in milk, oil and vanilla. Mix boiling water and chocolate syrup. Pour over batter. Place small trivet or band from canning jar in bottom of cooker, add 2 cups warm water. Place mold in cooker and cover with 4 layers of paper towels. Cover cooker and cook on high 3 to 4 hours. Serve warm with cream.

PUMPKIN BREAD

* 1 cup all-purpose flour
* 1 1/2 tsp baking powder
* 1 tsp pumpkin pie spice
* 1/2 cup brown sugar, firmly packed
* 2 Tb vegetable oil
* 2 eggs
* 1/2 cup pumpkin (canned)
* 4 Tb raisins or dried currants, finely chopped

In small bowl combine flour, baking powder and pumpkin pie spice; set aside.

In med. mixing bowl combine brown sugar and oil; beat till well combined. Beat in eggs. Add pumpkin; mix well. Add flour mixture. Beat just until combined. Stir in raisins. Pour pumpkin mixture into 2 well-greased and floured 1/2-pint straight-sided canning jars. Cover jars tightly with greased foil. Place a piece of crumpled foil in 3-1/2 or 4 qt. crockery cooker with liner in place. Place jars atop crumpled foil.

Cover; cook on high setting for 1-1/2 to 1-3/4 hours or until a wooden toothpick inserted near centers comes out clean. Remove jars from cooker; cool 10 minutes in jars. Remove bread from jars. Cool thoroughly on wire rack. Makes 2 loaves.

PUMPKIN TEA BREAD
   * 1/2 c. oil
   * 1/2 c. sugar
   * 1/2 c. brown sugar
   * 2 beaten eggs
   * 1 c. canned pumpkin
   * 1 1/2 c. sifted flour
   * 1/2 tsp. salt
   * 1/2 tsp. cinnamon
   * 1/2 tsp. nutmeg
   * 1 tsp. soda
   * 1 c. chopped walnuts

Blend oil and two sugars. Stir in beaten eggs and pumpkin. Sift dry ingredients together. Add and then stir in nuts. Pour batter into greased and floured 1 lb. 10 oz. coffee can. Place can in Crock Pot. Cover top of can with 6-8 paper towels; place lid on top. Bake on high 2 1/2 - 3 1/2 hours. No fair peeking until last hour.

RED RICE
   * 4 to 6 slices bacon, fried & crumbled
   * 1 large onion, coarsely chopped
   * 2 cans chopped tomatoes, (15 oz each)
   * 1 cup converted rice
   * 1/2 to 1 cup cooked chopped ham
   * salt and pepper, to taste
   * 1/8 teaspoon hot pepper sauce, or to taste

Fry bacon; drain and crumble. Cook onion in bacon grease just until softened. Combine all ingredients in the slow cooker/Crock Pot. Cover and cook on low for 6 to 7 hours, or until rice is tender but not mushy.
   Serves 6 to 8

REFRIED BEAN DIP
   * 1 (20 oz can) refried beans
   * 1/4 teaspoon salt

* 1 cup shredded cheddar cheese
* 1 (4 oz can) chopped green chiles
* 2 tablespoons bottled taco sauce
* 1/2 cup chopped green onions
* tortilla chips

In Crock Pot combine beans with cheese, chiles, onions, salt, and taco sauce. Cover and cook on low for 2 to 2-1/2 hours. Serve hot from the pot.

REUBEN DIP

* 1 small can sauerkraut
* 1 (8 oz.) cream cheese
* 1 (6 oz.) shredded Swiss cheese
* 6 ounces diced corned beef
* 2 tbsp. Thousand Island Dressing

Drain and rinse sauerkraut, mix with cream cheese and Swiss cheese. Add diced corned beef and Thousand Island dressing. Cover and heat on low until cheeses are melted, stirring occasionally to blend all ingredients. Serve warm with crackers or cocktail rye bread.

RHUBARB BAKE

* 1 3/4 cup fresh rhubarb
* 3/4 cup sugar
* 1 cinnamon stick
* 2 whole cloves
* 1 teaspoon grated lemon peel
* 1/4 cup butter or margarine
* 1/3 cup flour
* 1/3 cup sugar

Cut rhubarb into small pieces. Combine rhubarb with 3/4 cup sugar, cinnamon, cloves and lemon peel in cooker. Cover and cook on low for 3 to 4 hours. Remove whole spices. Spoon rhubarb into baking dish. Combine remaining ingredients and sprinkle over rhubarb. Bake at 400 degrees for 20 to 25 minutes.

Serves 4 to 6.

RICE PUDDING

* 2 1/2 c. cooked rice
* 1 1/2 c. scalded milk

* 2/3 c. white or brown sugar
* 3 eggs, beaten
* 1 tsp. salt
* 2 tbsp. vanilla
* 1 tsp. cinnamon
* 1 tsp. nutmeg
* 1/2 c. raisins
* 3 tbsp. soft butter

Combine all ingredients. Pour into lightly greased Crock Pot. Cook on high 1 to 2 hours. Stir during first 30 minutes. Recipe can be doubled.

RICE PUDDING WITH FRUIT

1/2 gallon milk*
1 cup uncooked rice
1 cup sugar
3 tablespoons cold margarine
1/4 teaspoon salt, optional
1 teaspoon vanilla extract
1/2 cup dried apricots or peaches, minced
1/4 teaspoon ground cinnamon

*Use half nonfat and half whole milk or all nonfat for lower fat content. Can substitute evaporated milk for a very rich flavor.

The cooking time will vary greatly, anywhere from 1 1/2 to 3 1/2 hours. The longer it cooks, the thicker it will be. It is important to have the dried apricots minced. Put all ingredients into the slow cooker/Crock Pot. Stir to blend well. Cover and cook on high for 1 1/2 hours; stir once after about an hour. Or, cook on high for the first 30 minutes, turn to low and cook as long as desired. Check after the first 2 hours of low cooking and stir. If the rice is not absorbing the milk quickly enough, turn the slow cooker/Crock Pot up to high again. Keep cover on at all times.

Slow Cooker temperatures vary widely among different brands. Only experimentation can tell you the correct amount of time for cooking in your slow cooker/Crock Pot. Rarely will a slow cooker/Crock Pot recipe fail, though, as the long, slow cooking process does not require precise timing.

Serves 8.

RICH BROWNIES IN A NUT CRUST
1/4 cup butter or margarine, melted
1 cup chopped nuts
1 family-size package brownie mix (about 23 oz.)
Pour melted butter into 2-pound coffee can; swirl to butter sides. Sprinkle with half the nuts. Mix brownies according to the package directions. Pour half the batter into coffee can, covering nuts evenly. Add remaining half of nuts, then batter. Place can in Crock-Pot. Cover top of can with 8 paper towels. Cover and bake on High setting for 3 hours. Do not check or remove cover until last hour. (If using Bread 'n Cake Bake pan, bake in covered pan on High setting for 2 to 3 hours.) Remove can and discard paper towels. Let stand 5 minutes. Unmold and serve warm.
24 brownies (for 3 1/2- or 5-quart Crock-Pot).

RICOTTA AMARETTO CHEESECAKE
Crust:
1 cup vanilla wafer crumbs (about 21 to 23 cookies)
1 tablespoon sugar
1/8 teaspoon almond extract
3 tablespoons butter
Filling:
15 ounces light ricotta cheese
8 ounces cream cheese
2/3 cup sugar
3 large eggs plus 1 egg yolk
1/4 cup Amaretto liqueur
2 tablespoons all-purpose flour
1/4 teaspoon almond extract
1/2 teaspoon vanilla extract
Combine crust ingredients well; pat into a 7-inch springform pan. Beat sugar into the cheeses; add eggs; beat for 2 to 3 minutes on medium speed of an electric hand-held mixer. Add remaining filling ingredients and beat about 2 minutes more. Pour into prepared crust. Place the cheesecake on a rack in the Crock Pot (or use a "ring" of aluminum foil to keep it off the bottom of the pot). Cover and cook on high for 2 1/2 to 3 hours. Let stand in the covered pot (after turning it

off) for about 1 to 2 hours, until cool enough to handle. Cool thoroughly before removing pan sides. Chill before serving; store leftovers in the refrigerator.

ROASTED VEGGIE TRIO POT
3 cups (15 oz) sliced raw potatoes
3 cups sliced carrots
1-3/4 cups (one 15 oz can) Swanson Beef Broth
1/2 cup chopped onions
In a slow cooker, combine potatoes, carrots and onion. Pour beef broth evenly over top. Cover and cook on HIGH for 4 - 6 hours. Mix well before serving.

RUSSIAN CHICKEN
* 1 bottle Russian dressing (16 oz.)
* 1 envelope onion soup mix
* 1 jar apricot preserves (10 oz.)
* 4 pieces chicken -- (4 to 6)
* Seasoned salt and pepper to taste
Combine dressing, preserves and onion soup mix in bowl and pour into a slow cooker/Crock Pot. Sprinkle chicken with seasoned salt and pepper. Place chicken, skin side down, in slow cooker/Crock Pot. Cook on LOW for 8 hours (HIGH 4 hours)
Serves 4 - 6.

SALMON AND POTATO CASSEROLE
* 4 potatoes, peeled and thinly sliced
* 3 tablespoons flour
* salt and pepper
* 1 can (16 ounces) salmon, drained and flaked
* 1 medium onion, chopped
* 1 can (10 3/4 ounces) cream of mushroom soup
* 1/4 cup water
* nutmeg
Place half of the potatoes in greased slow cooker/Crock Pot. Sprinkle with half of the flour, salt and pepper. Cover with half the salmon; sprinkle with half the onion. Repeat layers in order. Combine

soup and water. Pour over potato-salmon mixture. Dust with nutmeg.
Cover and cook on Low for 7-10 hours.
Serves 6.

SALMON BAKE IN CROCKPOT
* 3 cans Salmon, 1 lb each
* 4 cups Bread crumbs, soft 10 slices
* 1 can Tomatoes in puree, 1 lb.
* 1 Green pepper, chopped
* 3 teaspoons Lemon juice
* 1 can Cream of onion soup, cond.
* 2 Chicken bouillon cubes, crushed
* 6 Eggs, well beaten
* 1 can Cream of celery soup, cond.
* 1/2 cup Milk

Grease removable liner well. Combine all ingredients, except
celery soup and milk, in removable liner. Place liner in base. Cover
and cook on low 4-6 hours or auto for 3 hours. Combine cream of
celery soup with 1/2 cup of milk and heat in saucepan. Use as sauce
for salmon bake.

SAVORY SALSA-CORN CAKE
* 2 boxes corn muffin mix, (8 oz each)
* 1 can creamed corn, (15 ounce)
* 2 eggs
* 1/2 cup sour cream
* 1 can chopped green chiles, (4 ounces) undrained
* 2 tablespoons soft margarine
* 3 to 4 Tbs chunky salsa

In a medium bowl, combine creamed corn, eggs, sour cream,
chiles, and margarine. Whisk together until well combined. Add corn
muffin mix, stirring well to combine. Generously grease a 3 1/2-quart
slow cooker/Crock Pot with margarine or butter. Pour batter into the
slow cooker/Crock Pot. Spoon salsa over the top and cut into the
batter. Cover and cook on high for about 2 1/2 hours. Turn heat off
and let cool with lid ajar, for about 15 minutes. Loosen sides with a
knife and invert onto a large plate. If a little of the top sticks to the
bottom of the pot, dollop a little salsa on the top, or decorate with
sour cream and chopped green onion.

Delicious side dish!
Serves 6 to 8.

SCALLOPED CORN
3 large eggs
1 cup half and half
1 Tablespoon sugar
1/4 teaspoon salt
1/4 teaspoon pepper
3 to 4 tablespoons minced onion
2 cups frozen creamed corn, thawed
1 cup coarsely crushed cracker crumbs

Wisk milk and eggs together, then mix in remaining ingredients. Pour into lightly buttered casserole which will fit in the slow cooker/Crock Pot. Cover and cook on high for 2 1/2 hours, or until knife inserted in center comes out clean.

Serves 6 as a side dish.

SCALLOPED POTATO-TOMATO POT
6 cups (20 oz) frozen shredded hash browns
2 cups (one 16 oz can) cut green beans, rinsed and drained
1/4 cup finely chopped onion
1 teaspoon dried parsley flakes
1 (10-3/4 oz) can Healthy Request Cream of Celery Soup
1-3/4 cups (one 14-1/2 oz can) stewed tomatoes, undrained

In a slow cooker, combine hash browns, green beans and onion. In a medium bowl, combine parsley flakes, celery soup and undrained stewed tomatoes. Add soup mixture to potato mixture. Mix well to combine. Cover and cook on LOW for 6 - 8 hours. Mix well before serving.

SCALLOPED POTATOES
10 large Potatoes, thin slice
2 large Onions, chopped
2 cans Cheddar cheese soup, cond.
1 cup Milk

In a small bowl, combine soup with milk. In removable liner, layer one half the potatoes and one half the chopped onions; spread one half the soup-milk mixture. Repeat layering using rest of ingredients. Placed in base. Cover and cook on low for 6-8 hours, high for 3-4 hours or auto for 5 hours.

SCALLOPED POTATOES WITH HAM
1/2 cup diced ham
8 to 10 med. potatoes, thinly sliced
1 c. grated American cheese
Salt and pepper
1 can cream of mushroom soup, or 1 cup medium white sauce
Paprika
1 onion, thinly sliced

In slow cooker/Crock Pot layer half of ham, half of potatoes, half of onions, half of cheese. Sprinkle with salt and pepper. Repeat layers with remaining half of ingredients. Spoon undiluted soup or white sauce over top and sprinkle with paprika. Cover and cook on low for 7 to 9 hours.

SHRIMP CREOLE
1 1/2 c diced celery
1 1/4 c chopped onion
3/4 c chopped bell pepper
1 (8oz) can tomato sauce
1 (28 oz) can whole tomatoes
1 clove garlic*
1 tsp salt
1/4 tsp pepper
6 drops Tabasco sauce (optional)
1 lb shrimp, deveined and shelled

Combine all ingredients except shrimp. Cook 3 - 4 hours on high or 6 - 8 hours on low. Add shrimp last hour of cooking. Serve over hot rice. Chicken, rabbit or crawfish may be substituted for the shrimp. * 1 tsp garlic salt or 1/4 tsp garlic powder may be substituted.

SHRIMP MARINARA
* 1 (16 oz.) can of tomatoes, cut up
* 2 tbsp. minced parsley
* 1 clove of garlic, minced
* 1/2 tsp. dried basil

* 1 tsp. salt
* 1/4 tsp. pepper
* 1 tsp. dried oregano
* 1 (6 oz.) can tomato paste
* 1/2 tsp. seasoned salt
* 1 lb. cooked shelled shrimp
* Grated Parmesan cheese
* Cooked spaghetti

In a Crock Pot, combine tomatoes with parsley, garlic, basil, salt, pepper, oregano, tomato paste and seasoned salt. Cover and cook on low for 6 to 7 hours. Turn control to high, stir in shrimp, cover and cook on high for 10 to 15 minutes more.

Serve over cooked spaghetti. Top with Parmesan cheese.

SIMPLE SAUCY POTATOES
* 4 cans (15 ounces each)sliced white potatoes , drained
* 2 cans condensed cream of celery soup , undiluted
* 2 cups sour cream
* 10 bacon strips, cooked and crumbled
* 6 green onions , thinly sliced

Place potatoes in slow cooker. Combine the remaining ingredients; pour over the potatoes and mix well. Cover and cook on high for 4-5 hours.

SLOW-COOKED BROCCOLI
2 packages (10 oz. each) frozen chopped broccoli, partially thawed

1 can (10-3/4 oz.) condensed cream of celery soup, undiluted

1-1/2 cups shredded sharp cheddar cheese, divided

1/4 cup chopped onion

1/2 teaspoon Worchestershire sauce

1/4 teaspoon pepper

1 cup crushed butter-flavored crackers(about 25)

2 tablespoons butter or margarine

In a large bowl, combine broccoli, soup, 1 cup cheese, onion, Worcestershire sauce and pepper.

Pour into a greased slow cooker. Sprinkle crackers on top; dot with butter. Cover and cook on high for 2-1/2 to 3 hours. Sprinkle with remaining cheese. Cook 10 minutes longer or until the cheese is melted.

Yield: 8-10 servings.

SLOW-COOKED CORN PUDDING
1/4 cup chopped onion
1/4 cup chopped green pepper
1/4 cup chopped fresh tomato
1 16 oz can cream-style corn
4 large eggs
1/2 cup evaporated milk
1/2 teaspoon salt
1/4 teaspoon pepper

Saute onion and green pepper until slightly softened; add tomato and saute for 1 minute more.

In a medium-sized bowl, whisk together the eggs, milk, creamed corn and seasonings; add the sauteed vegetables. Lightly grease a 3 1/2 quart Crock Pot (or a souffle dish which fits in a larger Crock Pot) and pour the mixture in. Cook on high 2 1/2 to 3 hours; add grated cheese to the top and cook until cheese is melted.

SLOW-COOKER CANDY
* 2 lbs. white almond bark
* 4 oz. bar German chocolate
* 12 oz. pkg. semi-sweet chocolate chips
* 24 oz. jar dry roasted peanuts

Put all ingredients in Crock Pot; cook 1 hour on high. Do not stir. Turn Crock Pot to low and stir every 15 minutes for 1 hour.

Drop on waxed paper and cool. Store in an air-tight container.

SLOW-COOKER CREAMY CORN
* 1 large Bag frozen corn
* 8 ounces Pkg. cream cheese
* 1 Stick margarine
* Salt and pepper to taste

Melt cream cheese and margarine in microwave. Spray slow cooker/Crock Pot with vegetable spray. Put melted cream cheese and margarine in slow cooker/Crock Pot. Add corn, salt and pepper. Cook in slow cooker/Crock Pot for two hours on low.

SLOW-COOKER CREAMY SCALLOPED POTATOES AND HAM
3 lbs. med. size potatoes peeled and sliced
1 onion chopped
1 cup shredded cheddar cheese
1 cup cooked ham
1 can (10 3/4 oz) reduced fat cream of mushroom soup
1/2 cup water
Combine potatoes, onion, cheese and ham in slow cooker/Crock Pot. In small bowl, stir together soup & water. Pour over potato mixture. Cover pot. Cook on High for 4 hours or until potatoes are tender. Stir mixture just before serving. Makes 6 servings

SLOW-COOKER SEAFOOD CHOWDER
* 2 lbs. frozen fish filets
* 1/4 lb. bacon or salt pork, diced
* 1 medium onion, chopped
* 4 medium potatoes, peeled and cubed
* 2 cups water
* 1 1/2 tsp. salt (unless you are using fresh salt-water fish)
* 1/4 tsp. pepper
* 1 can evaporated milk
Thaw frozen fish in refrigerator. Cut into bite-sized pieces. In skillet, saute bacon or salt pork and onion until meat is cooked and onion is golden. Drain and put into Crock Pot with the fish pieces. Add potatoes, water, salt and pepper. Cover and cook on low for 6 - 9 hours. Add evaporated milk during last hour. If the chowder is thicker than you like, add more milk (any kind).

SLOW-COOKER SHRIMP CREOLE
* 1 1/2 c. diced celery
* 1 1/4 c. chopped onion
* 3/4 c. chopped bell pepper
* 1 (8 oz.) can tomato sauce
* 1 (28 oz.) can whole tomatoes
* 1 clove garlic*
* 1 tsp. salt

* 1/4 tsp. pepper
* 6 drops Tabasco (opt.)
* 1 lb. shrimp, deveined & shelled

*1 teaspoon garlic salt or 1/4 teaspoon garlic powder may be substituted. Combine all ingredients except shrimp. Cook 3 to 4 hours on high or 6 to 8 hours on low. Add shrimp last hour of cooking. Serve over hot rice. Chicken, rabbit or crawfish may be substituted for shrimp. Stove top version, if you don't have a Crock Pot. Saute celery, onion and bell peppers in oil or butter until tender. (Better if left

a bit crunchy.) Add remaining ingredients except meat being used. Simmer at least 30 minutes to an hour. Add shrimp or whatever meat you wish and simmer 30 minutes more. This is even better reheated the next day.

SOUTHERN STYLE GREEN BEAN & POTATO CASSEROLE

4 to 6 medium red potatoes, sliced about 1/4" thick (peeled or not)

4 to 5 cups whole fresh green beans, trimmed
6 slices bacon, diced fried and drained
2 tablspoons minced dried onion
1 can 98% fat free cream of celery soup
salt and pepper to taste

Place sliced potatoes and green beans in slow cooker/Crock Pot; add other ingredients. Cover and cook on low 7 to 9 hours.

Serves 4 to 6.

SOUR CREAM CHILI BAKE

1 pound Ground beef
1 can Pinto beans, drained (15 oz)
1 can Enchilada sauce (10 oz)
1 can Tomato sauce (8 oz)
1 cup Shredded process Amer cheese
1 tablespoon Instant minced onion
1 cup Water
4 cups Corn chips
1 cup Sour cream
1/2 cup Shredded process American cheese

Brown ground beef; drain. Transfer meat to Crock Pot. Stir in beans, enchilada sauce, tomato sauce, 1 cup of cheese, onion and 1 cup of water. Reserve 1 cup of corn chips; crush the remaining chips and add to the meat mixture. Cover and cook on low heat for 8 to 10 hours. To serve, top with sour cream, remaining cheese, and reserved corn chips.

SPAGHETTI SAUCE WITH CHICKEN & SAUSAGE
* 1 lb. Italian sausage
* 3-4 boneless chicken breasts, cut into 1-inch chunks
* 1 cup chopped green pepper
* 1 cup chopped onion
* 1-2 tsp. Italian seasoning
* 2 (4 oz. each) cans mushroom stems and pieces, drained
* 2 jars favorite spaghetti sauce
* Hot cooked pasta

In skillet, brown Italian sausage, piercing casings to allow excess fat to run out.

Remove to plate and cut into 1/2 to 1-inch chunks.

In same skillet, brown chicken pieces. (I like to sauté the pepper and onion a bit, too.) Place sausage and chicken in slow cooker. Add pepper and onion. Sprinkle with Italian seasoning. Add mushrooms. Pour sauce over everything. Cover and cook on low for 6 to 8 hours. Stir before serving over spaghetti or other pasta.

SPAGHETTI SQUASH
2 cups water
1 spaghetti squash, a size which will fit in slow cooker/Crock Pot

With a skewer or large fork, puncture several holes in the squash. Pour water in the slow cooker/Crock Pot, add the whole squash. Cover and cook on low for 8 to 9 hours. Split and remove seeds, then transfer the "spaghetti" strands to a bowl. Serve tossed with butter and salt and pepper, Parmesan cheese or your favorite sauce.

SPANISH CHICKEN
2 lb. boneless skinless chicken breast
Seasoned salt & pepper to taste

Black olives, pitted
Sliced mushrooms, drained
Stewed tomatoes
Liquid to cover (beer, tomato soup or tomato sauce w/equal amount of
water or stock)
Cut chicken into bite-sized pieces; season. Place with remaining ingredients in slow cooker. Simmer all day on low. Serve over rice.
Serves 4.

SPICY CHICKEN WINGS

* 3 tbsp. vinegar
* 24 chicken wings, drummettes
* 1/4 c. hot pepper sauce, or less
* 1/2 c. melted butter
* 1 pkg. Hidden Valley Ranch original dry salad dressing mix

Preheat oven to 350 degrees. Mix all ingredients together except chicken wings and salad dressing mix. Place chicken wings in baking dish or pan in a single layer. Pour mixture over wings. Sprinkle with dry dressing mix. Bake 25 - 30 minutes or until browned. Sprinkle with paprika if you like. Chicken wings may be made in slow cooker/Crock Pot - cook on low 4 to 5 hours.

SPICY FRANKS

* 1 cup ketchup
* 1/4 cup brown sugar, packed
* 1 tablespoon red wine vinegar
* 2 teaspoons soy sauce
* 2 teaspoons Dijon mustard
* 1/8 teaspoon garlic powder
* 1 pound hot dogs, cut into bite-size pieces, or cocktail wieners, smoked sausage, etc.

Combine everything but hot dogs in the Crock Pot; cover and cook on high 1 to 2 hours, until well blended. Add hot dogs, stir, and cook another 1 to 2 hours, until heated through. Turn to low to keep warm and serve from the Crock Pot.

SPICY MARMALADE MEATBALLS

Meatballs:

* 2 lbs ground beef (chuck)
* 1/2 cup bread crumbs
* 1 teaspoon Worcestershire sauce
* 1/2 teaspoon salt
* 1/4 teaspoon pepper
* 1 small onion, minced
* 1/2 teaspoon chili powder
* 1/4 teaspoon garlic powder
* 3 eggs
Sauce:
* 2 cups ketchup
* 1/4 cup Worcestershire sauce
* 1 jar orange marmalade (10 to 12 ounces)
* dash cayenne, more or less to taste
* 1 teaspoon chili powder

Combine sauce ingredients in slow cooker/Crock Pot; cover and cook on high while preparing meatballs. Combine meatball ingredients. Heat a large skillet over medium high heat. Add meatballs; brown on all sides. You might have to do this in batches. Place browned meatballs in a 325° oven and bake for 45 minutes (if the skillet isn't ovenproof, transfer to a baking dish). Transfer meatballs to slow cooker/Crock Pot with a slotted spoon or drain on brown paper first. Cover and reduce to LOW for 2 to 4 hours. Serve hot as an appetizer or over rice for a main dish. Makes 24 to 48 meatballs, depending on size.

SPICY REFRIED BEAN DIP
* 2 cans refried beans, (16ounce each)
* 1 package taco seasoning mix, about 1 1/4 oz
* 1/2 cup chopped onion
* 2 cups Monterey jack cheese, shredded
* a few drops Tabasco sauce, to taste
* chopped jalapeno or mild chiles, to taste

Place refried beans, taco seasoning, onion, cheese, and Tabasco sauce in the slow cooker/Crock Pot; stir well. Stir in chopped chiles. Cover and cook on low until cheese is melted, about 1 hour; add a little water if mixture seems too thick. Serve from the slow cooker/Crock Pot with French bread, crackers, or chips.

Makes about 4 cups.

SPINACH, CHEESE & BACON STRATA
4 cups sliced & buttered French bread, cubed
1 bag frozen spinach (16 oz)
6 to 8 ounces diced, cooked bacon, ham, or turkey ham
1 1/2 to 2 cups shredded cheddar cheese
salt and pepper, to taste
1 can (10oz) cream of mushroom soup (the 98% fat free is fine)
1/2 cup evaporated milk
5 eggs
1 tablespoon minced dried onion (optional)

Lightly butter a 3 1/2-quart slow cooker/Crock Pot. Layer with half of the buttered bread cubes, spinach, bacon, and cheese; salt and pepper to taste. Repeat layers ending with cheese. Whisk together the soup, milk, eggs, and dried onion. Pour over slow cooker/Crock Pot mixture. Chill for 1 hour or overnight. Cover and cook on low for 3 1/2 to 4 1/2 hours. Serves 4 to 6.

SPINACH SOUFFLE
2 pounds frozen spinach, thawed and drained
1/4 cup grated onion
1 8 oz pkg light cream cheese, softened
1/2 cup mayonnaise
1/2 cup shredded Cheddar cheese
2 eggs, beaten
1/4 teaspoon white or black pepper
dash nutmeg

Mix thawed and drained spinach together with onion. Beat remaining ingredients and blend in spinach mixture. Spoon mixture into a lightly buttered 3 1/2-quart Crock Pot (or souffle dish to fit in a larger crock pot) and cook on high for 2 to 3 hours.

SPOON PEACHES
1/3 cup sugar
1/2 cup brown sugar
2 tsp. margarine, melted
1/2 can evaporated milk

3/4 cup Bisquik
2 eggs
2 cups peaches, mashed
2 tsp. vanilla
3/4 tsp. cinnamon
Spray slow cooker/Crock Pot with non-stick cooking spray. Combine sugars and Bisquik. Add eggs and vanilla.

Add margarine and milk. Add peaches and cinnamon. Pour into slow cooker/Crock Pot. Cook on low for 6 to 8 hours.

SQUASH CASSEROLE I
5 cups yellow squash, canned or frozen
1/2 cup butter or margarine, melted
1 can cream of chicken soup
2 slices cubed bread
1 cup sour cream
Place squash in slow cooker with butter and cook for 1 hour. Add soup as it comes from the can, and cook until hot. Add bread and sour cream and cook until bubbly.

SQUASH CASSEROLE II
2 pounds yellow summer squash or zucchini, thinly sliced (about 6 cups)
1/2 medium onion, chopped
1 cup pared shredded carrot
1 can (10 1/4 ounces) condensed cream of chicken soup
1 cup sour cream
1/4 cup flour
1 package (8 ounces) seasoned stuffing crumbs
1/2 cup butter or margarine, melted
In large bowl, combine squash, onion, carrot and soup. Mix sour cream and flour, stir into vegetables. Toss stuffing crumbs with butter and place half in slow cooker/Crock Pot. Add vegetable mixture and top with remaining stuffing crumbs. Cover and cook on LOW for 6-8 hrs.
Serves 4 to 6.

STEWED TOMATOES
6 to 8 ripe tomatoes

2 tablespoons margarine
1 medium onion, thinly sliced
3/4 cup chopped celery
1/2 cup chopped green pepper
3 tablespoons sugar (more or less)
1 small bay leaf
1 teaspoon salt
1/8 teaspoon pepper

Core tomatoes; place in boiling water for about 15 to 20 seconds, then into ice water to cool quickly; peel. Cut tomatoes in wedges. In Crock Pot, combine all ingredients. Cover and cook on low 8-9 hours. Remove bay leaf. Sprinkle top with parsley, if desired. Serve as a side dish or freeze in portions for soups or other recipes.
Serves 6.

STREUSEL POUND CAKE

1 pkg. pound cake mix (16 oz.) size
1/4 c. packed brown sugar
1 tbsp. flour
1/4 c. finely chopped nuts
1 tsp. cinnamon

Mix cake mix according to package directions. Pour batter into well greased and floured 2 pound coffee tin. Combine sugar, flour, nuts and cinnamon and sprinkle over cake batter. Place can in crock-pot. Cover top of can with 8 layers of paper towels. Cover pot and bake on high 3 to 4 hours.

STUFFED GREEN PEPPERS

1 package (10 oz) frozen corn kernels
1 can (15 oz) red kidney beans drained and rinsed
1 can (14.5 oz) diced tomatoes
1/4 cup salsa
1/4 cup chopped onions
1 1/2 cups cooked rice
1 tsp Worcestershire sauce
1/4 tsp salt
1/2 tsp pepper
2 cups shredded reduced fat Cheddar cheese, divided
6 green peppers. tops removed & seeded

Combine all ingredients, except 1/4 cup cheese and green peppers. Stuff peppers. Arrange peppers in Crock Pot. Cover, cook on low 6 - 8 hours (high 3 - 4 hours) Sprinkle with 1/4 cup cheese during the last 30 minutes.

Makes 6 servings

STUFFED POTATOES
* 6 baking potatoes, washed
* 3 tbsp butter
* 1 cup milk
* chopped chives
* 1 tsp salt
* 1//8 tsp pepper
* 3 tbls Parmesan cheese
* shredded cheddar cheese

Place damp potatoes in bottom of cooker. Cover and cook on low for 6 to 8 hours. Remove and cut a slice, lengthwise, from each potato. Scoop out insides. Save shell. Add remaining ingredients and beat until fluffy. Spoon mixture back into shells and top each with shredded cheddar cheese. Bake at 425 degrees for 15 minutes or until cheese is melted and bubbly.

Serves 6.

SUGARED PECANS
* 16 ounces pecan halves
* 1/2 cup butter, melted
* 1/2 cup powdered sugar
* 1 1/2 teaspoons ground cinnamon
* 1/4 teaspoon ground ginger
* 1/4 teaspoon ground allspice

Stir the pecans and butter in a 3 1/2-quart Crock Pot until combined. Add powdered sugar, stirring to coat. Cover and cook on high for 15 minutes. Turn to low and cook uncovered for about 2 hours, or until the nuts are covered with a crisp glaze. Transfer to a bowl, combine spices and sift over nuts, tossing to distribute evenly. Cool before serving.

SUGARED WALNUTS & PECANS
* 1 pound Pecans or Walnut pieces

* 1/2 cup Unsalted butter - melted
* 1/2 cup Powdered sugar
* 1/4 tsp Allspice - ground
* 1/8 tsp Cloves - ground
* 1 1/2 tsp Cinnamon - ground
* 1/4 tsp Ginger - ground
- - Preheat slow cooker/Crock Pot on high for 15 minutes.
- - First, in preheated slow cooker/Crock Pot stir the walnuts (or pecans) and butter until mixed well.
- - Add the powdered sugar, stirring to coat evenly.
- - Cover and slow-cook on high for 15 minutes.
- - Reduce the heat to low and slow cook, UNCOVERED, stirring occasionally, until the nuts are coated with a crisp glaze (should be about 2 hours.)
- - Transfer the nuts to a bowl.
- - In another small bowl, combine the spices and sift them over the nuts, stirring to coat evenly.
- - Let cool before serving.

SUN-DRIED TOMATO SPAGHETTI SAUCE
1 1/2 cups chopped sun-dried tomatoes
1 medium onion, chopped
1 cup celery, chopped
2 cloves garlic, minced
36 oz whole or chopped tomatoes, undrained
2/3 cup chablis or other dry white wine 1
teaspoon dried fennel seed
1 1/2 tsp. basil
1/2 teaspoon oregano
1/2 teaspoon pepper
Salt to taste
Place all ingredients in slow cooker/Crock Pot and cook on low for 6-8 hours.
Note: You can add mushrooms if desired.

SUNSHINE SQUASH
1 butternut squash, about 2 pounds, peeled, seeded and diced
1 can(14-1/2-ounce) tomatoes, undrained
1 can(about 15-ounces) corn, drained

1 medium onion, coarsley chopped
1 clove garlic, minced well
1 green bell pepper, seeded and cut into 1-" pieces
1 canned green chili, coarsely chopped
1/2 cup chicken broth
1/2 teaspoon salt
1/4 teaspoon black pepper
1 tablespoon plus 1-1/2- teaspoons tomato paste
Combine all ingredients except tomato paste in slow-cooker. Cover and cook on LOW 6 hours or until squash is tender. Remove about 1/4- cup cooking liquid and blend with tomato paste. Stir into slow-cooker. Cook 30 minutes or until mixture is slightly thickened and heated through. Serves 6- 8.

SWEET AND SOUR CABBAGE

4 bacon slices, diced
1/4 cup packed
brown sugar
2 tbsp. all-purpose flour
1/2 tsp. salt
1/8 tsp. pepper
1/4 cup water
1/4 cup vinegar
1 medium head red cabbage, shredded(about
8 cups)
1 small onion finely chopped
In a skillet, cook bacon until crisp; reserve drippings. Combine 1 tbsp. drippings in a slow cooker with remaining ingredients, except cooked bacon. Cover and cook on LOW 6 1/2 to 7 hours or until cabbage is tender. Spoon into serving bowl; sprinkle with reserved bacon.

SWEET 'N' SOUR CHICKEN

6 med. carrots, cut into 1/2" chunks
1/2 c. finely chopped green pepper
1 sm. onion, finely chopped
3 split chicken breasts (remove skin, optional)
1/2 tsp. salt
1 (10 oz.) jar Sweet N Sour sauce

1 (15 oz.) can pineapple chunks, drained
2 tbsp. cornstarch
Place all ingredients in slow cooker/Crock Pot with chicken on top. Cover and cook on low 6-8 hours. Remove chicken and thicken with 2 tablespoons cornstarch dissolved to a medium thick paste with water. Pour over chicken breasts - or remove chicken from bone and come with sauce mixture. Serve with steamed white or brown rice.

SWEET AND SOUR FRANKS
* 1 cup chili sauce
* 1 cup currant jelly
* 3 tablespoons lemon juice
* 1 tablespoon prepared mustard
* 2 pounds cocktail franks or hot dogs cut into bite-sized pieces
* 2 cans Pineapple chunks, 27 ozs
Combine first four ingredients in Crock Pot; mix well to break up jelly chunks. Cover and cook on high 15 to 20 minutes to soften jelly and blend sauce ingredients. Add cut-up hot dogs or cocktail franks. Add pineapple. Cover and cook on high for 2 hours; or low for 4 hours. Keep on low while serving.

SWEET AND SOUR KIELBASA
* 1 pound kielbasa
* 1 (10 oz.) jar red currant jelly
* 1/2 (5 oz.) jar golden spicy mustard (add whole jar for more spicy)
Cut kielbasa to bite-size pieces. Add to boiling water. Boil 8 to 10 minutes; poke with fork to release grease from meat. In slow cooker/Crock Pot, melt jelly on low heat. Add mustard. When kielbasa is done boiling, rinse, then add to slow cooker/Crock Pot mixture. Coat all of the meat. Simmer for 1 hour or more on low.

SWEET AND SOUR SAUSAGE BALLS
* 1/2 c. brown sugar
* 2 lbs. sausage
* 1 1/4 c. ketchup
* 1 tbsp. soy sauce
* 1 tbsp. lemon juice

* 1 can chunk pineapple

Roll sausage in balls, brown and add other ingredients. Cook until done in slow cooker.

SWEET AND SOUR SHRIMP

1 package (6 ox.) frozen Chinese pea pods, partially thawed

1 can (13 oz.) juice-pack pineapple chunks or tidbits (drain and reserve

juice)

2 tbls cornstarch

3 tbls sugar

1 chicken bouillon cube

1 cup boiling water

1/2 cup reserved pineapple juice

2 tsp soy sauce

1/2 tsp ground ginger

2 cans (4 1/2 oz. each) shrimp, rinsed & drained

2 tbls cider vinegar

Fluffy rice

Place pea pods and drained pineapple in Crock-Pot. In a small saucepan, stir together cornstarch and sugar. Dissolve bouillon cube in boiling water and add with juice, soy sauce and ginger to saucepan. Bring to a boil, stirring, and cook sauce for about 1 minute or until thickened and transparent. Gently blend sauce into pea pods and pineapple. Cover and cook on Low setting for 4 to 6 hours.

Before serving, add shrimp and vinegar, stirring carefully to avoid breaking up shrimp. Serve over hot rice.

4 to 5 servings (about 1 1/2 quarts)

SWEET POTATO AND PINEAPPLE PUDDING

3 pounds sweet potatoes, peeled and shredded

2 cans (8 oz.) crushed pineapple in unsweetened juice, undrained

1 can (12 oz.) evaporated milk

1 1/4 cups brown sugar, firmly packed

6 T. margarine or butter, cut in cubes

3 eggs, slightly beaten

1 t. ground cinnamon

1/2 t. nutmeg

Lightly grease Crock Pot. In Crock Pot, combine sweet potatoes, pineapple, evaporated milk, brown sugar, margarine, eggs, cinnamon, and nutmeg. Cover and cook on low 7-8 hours or on High 4 hours, stirring every 2 hours until the potatoes are tender. Serve hot or at room temperature.

NOTE: This dish may appear to be curdling, however it will come together toward the end of the cooking.

Serve 10 - 12. (This was for the 5 quart model).

SWEET POTATOES WITH APPLES

5 medium sweet potatoes

3 apples (such as Granny Smith) peeled & cored, cut in wedges

1/4 teaspoon Ground nutmeg

1/4 teaspoon ground cinnamon

1/4 cup Maple flavored syrup

2 tablespoons butter, melted

1/4 cup pecan pieces

Generously grease the bottom and sides of the slow cooker/Crock Pot with butter or margarine.

Peel sweet potatoes; cut into 1/2" slices. Place on bottom of slow cooker/Crock Pot. Top with apple wedges; then nutmeg and cinnamon, maple syrup, and the melted butter. Cover and cook on low about 4 hours or until potatoes are tender. Sprinkle with pecans the last 30 minutes.

Serves 4 to 6.

SWEET SWEET-POTATOES

2 pounds sweet potatoes---peel and grated

1/3 cup brown sugar---packed good

1/4 cup butter---melted

1/4 cup coconut---flaked

1/4 cup broken pecans---toasted

1/4 teaspoon cinnamon

1/4 teaspoon coconut extract

1/4 teaspoon vanilla

In a slow cooker/Crock Pot, combine potatoes, sugar, butter, coconut, pecans and cinnamon. Cover and cook on LOW for 6-8 hours or on HIGH for 3-4 hours. Stir in coconut and vanilla extracts.

SWISS CHEESE SCALLOPED POTATOES
* 2 pounds baking potatoes, peeled and thinly sliced
* 1/2 cup finely chopped yellow onion
* 1/4 tsp salt
* 1/4 tsp ground nutmeg
* 3 TBS butter, cut into 1/8-inch pieces
* 1/2 cup milk
* 2 TBS all-purpose flour
* 3 oz. Swiss cheese slices, torn into small pieces
* 1/4 cup finely chopped green onion (optional)

1. Layer half the potatoes, 1/4 cup onion, 1/8 tsp salt, 1/8 tsp nutmeg, 1 TBS butter in slow cooker. Repeat layers. Cover and cook on LOW 7 hours or on HIGH 4 hours. Remove potatoes with slotted spoon to serving dish.

2. Blend milk and flour in small bowl until smooth. Stir mixture into slow cooker. Add cheese; stir to combine. If slow cooker is on LOW, turn to HIGH, cover and cook until slightly thickened, about 10 minutes. Stir. Pour cheese mixture over potatoes and serve. Garnish with chopped green onions, if desired.

Makes 5 to 6 servings.

SWISS CHICKEN CASSEROLE
* 6 chicken breasts, boneless and skinless
* 6 slices Swiss cheese
* 1 can cream of mushroom soup
* 1/4 cup milk
* 2 cups stuffing mix
* 1/2 cup butter or margarine, melted

Lightly greas Crock Pot or spray with cooking spray. Place chicken breasts in pot. Top with cheese. Combine soup and milk, stirring well. Spoon over cheese; sprinkle with stuffing mix. Drizzle melted butter over stuffing mix. Cook on low 8 to 10 hours or high 4 to 6 hours.

Serves 6.

TACO CHILI
1 1/2 to 2 pounds lean ground beef

1 medium onion, chopped
1 pkg (1 1/4oz) taco seasoning mix
2 cans (14 1/2oz ea.) diced tomatoes
1 can (10oz) diced tomatoes with green chilies
1 can (16oz) pinto beans, rinsed and drained
1 15oz can chili beans in sauce
1 cup frozen whole kernel corn
Shredded cheese (mozzarella, Monterey Jack or
cheddar)
Slightly crushed tortilla chips

In a large skillet, cook ground beef and onion, one-half at a time, till meat is browned and onion is tender. Drain off fat. Transfer to a 3 1/2- to 5-quart crockery cooker. Stir in dry taco seasoning mix, diced tomatoes, diced tomatoes with green chilies, pinto beans, chili beans in chili sauce, and corn. Cover; cook on low for 8 to 10 hours or on high for 4 to 5 hours. Sprinkle each serving with some cheese and chips.

Makes 8 servings.

TEXAS CHILI
6 strips bacon
2 lbs. boneless beef cubes
2 cans (15 oz.) kidney beans, drained
1 can (28 oz.) tomatoes, cut up
1 can (8 oz.) tomato sauce
1 c. finely chopped onion
1/2 c. thinly sliced carrots
1/2 c. finely chopped green pepper
1/2 c. finely chopped celery
2 tbsp. minced parsley
2 cloves garlic minced
1 bay leaf
2 tbsp. chili powder
1 tsp. salt
1/8 tsp. pepper

Fry bacon until crisp. Remove bacon and drain on paper towel. Brown half the beef cubes in pan with bacon drippings five minutes. Place in slow cooker. Repeat with remaining meat. Stir bacon and remaining ingredients into 3 1/2 quart slow cooker. Cover and cook on low setting about 10 hours or until beef is tender. Stir occasionally. If you don't have a slow cooker place in large pot, cover, place on stove under low heat and follow directions above.

TERIYAKI SAUCE WINGS

* 3 pounds chicken wings
* 1 onion, chopped
* 1 cup soy sauce
* 1 cup brown sugar
* 2 teaspoons ground ginger
* 2 cloves garlic, crushed
* 1/4 cup dry sherry

Rinse chicken, and pat dry. Cut off wing tips and discard. Cut each wing into 2 pieces, cutting at the joint. Broil wings 4 inches from heat for about 10 minutes on each side, or until browned. Transfer to Crock Pot. Mix all remaining ingredients together and pour over chicken wings. Cook, covered, on low for 5 to 6 hours or on high for 2 to 3 hours. Stir once or twice to keep wings coated with sauce.

Makes about 32 wings.

TRIPLE CHOCOLATE MESS

1 package chocolate cake mix(any)
1 pint sour cream
1 pkg. instant chocolate pudding(any size)
1 6oz. bag chocolate chips
3/4 c. oil
4 eggs
1 c. water

Spray c.p. with non-stick spray. Mix all ingredients. Cook on low for 6-8 hours Try not to lift the lid.

Serve with ice cream.

I tried this with low fat cake mix, sour cream and fat free pudding. It turned out great! It is VERY rich, so be sure to have some ice cream in the house. A little goes a long way. Keeps in fridge for a while. Just heat and serve.

TUNA NOODLE CASSEROLE
    * 2 cans cream of celery soup
    * 1/3 cup dry sherry
    * 2/3 cup Milk
    * 2 tablespoons parsley flakes
    * 10 ounces frozen peas
    * 2 cans tuna, drained
    * 10 ounces egg noodles, cooked
    * 2 tablespoons butter or margarine
    * dash curry powder (optional)

In a large bowl, thoroughly combine soup, sherry, milk, parsley flakes, vegetables, and tuna. Fold in noodles. Pour into greased Crock Pot. Dot with butter or margarine. Cover and cook on Low 7 to 9 hours. (Cook noodles just until tender.)

TUNA SALAD CASSEROLE
2 cans tuna, drained and flaked
1 can cream of celery soup
4 hard-cooked eggs, chopped
1 cup diced celery
1/2 cup mayonnaise
1/4 tsp. pepper
1 1/2 cups crushed potato chips

Combine all ingredients except 1/4 cup of the crushed potato chips; stir well. Pour into greased Crock Pot. Top with remaining potato chips. Cover and cook on Low setting for 5-8 hours.

TURKEY AND RICE CASSEROLE
2 cans cream of mushroom soup
3 cups water
3 cups converted long-grain white rice (uncooked)
1 cup thinly sliced celery
1 to 2 cups cubed cooked turkey
2 cups frozen mixed vegetables (peas & carrots, oriental mix, etc.)
1 teaspoon poultry seasoning
1 tablespoon dried minced onion

Pour soup and water into Crock Pot and stir to combine. Add remaining ingredients and mix well. Cover and cook 6 to 8 hours on low or 3 to 4 hours on high. Add soy sauce if desired.

TURKEY BARBECUE

2 to 3 lb. turkey fillets
2 green peppers
1 teaspoon. celery salt
Dash of pepper
2 teaspoon. chopped onion
18 ounce thick barbecue sauce

Prepare turkey fillets with dash of pepper across tops. Bake in 350 degree oven for 1 hour covered.

Uncover for desired darker color. Prepare chopped green peppers, onions. Mix barbecue sauce, celery salt, (thin with water if needed) in 5 quart slow cooker/Crock Pot, set on high. Add green peppers and onions. Allow to heat while turkey is baking. Chop turkey (as desired in small tomedium chunks) and add to slow cooker/Crock Pot. Simmer for 2 to 3 hours, or turn to low and cook for 4 to 6 hours. Serve on fresh rolls.

Serves 4 to 6.

TURKEY MADEIRA

1 1/2 lb turkey breast tenders
2 ounce porcini mushrooms (dried)
3/4 cup chicken broth
3 tablespoons Madeira wine
1 tablespoon lemon juice
salt and pepper to taste

Cover and cook on low for 6 to 8 hours. Thicken juices with cornstarch if desired, and serve with rice.

Serves 4.

VEGETABLE BEEF SOUP

1 pound ground chuck
1 cup chopped onion
1 large (28 oz.) can whole tomatoes (chopped)
3 cup diced potatoes

1 (16 oz.) can cut green beans
2 teaspoon chili powder
2-3 dashes cayenne pepper sauce
2 (10 1/2 oz.) cans condensed beef bouillon
1 cup chopped celery
1 cup sliced carrots
1 teaspoon salt
1 teaspoon Worcestershire sauce
Brown meat with onion and celery; drain off fat. Stir in remaining ingredients and add 1 or 2 cups water. Cover and cook on low for 8-10 hours.

VEGETABLE CASSEROLE
* 2 cups carrots, cut in strips, cooked & drained
* 2 cups celery, diced
* 1 onion, diced
* 1/4 cup green pepper, diced
* 1 pint tomato juice
* 4 cups green beans, drained
* 1 teaspoon salt
* dash of pepper
* 3 tablespoons tapioca
* 1 tablespoon sugar
Mix all ingredients together in slow cooker/Crock Pot.
Dot with 2 tablespoons margarine and cook on low for 8-10 hour or on high for 4-5 hours.

VEGETABLE CURRY
* 4 medium Carrots, bias sliced into inch slices
* 2 medium Potatoes, cut into 1/2 cubes
* 15 ounces Can garbanzo beans, drained
* 8 ounces Green beans, cut into 1 pieces
* 1 cup Coarsely chopped onion
* 3 to 4 cloves Garlic, minced
* 2 tablespoons Quick-cooking tapioca
* 2 teaspoons Curry powder
* 1 teaspoon Ground coriander
* 1/2 teaspoon Crushed red pepper (opt'l)

* 1/4 teaspoon Salt
* 1/8 teaspoon Ground cinnamon
* 14 ounces Can vegetable broth
* 16 ounces Can tomatoes, cut up
* 2 cups Hot cooked rice

In a 3 1/2, 4, or 5 quart crockery cooker combine carrots, garbanzo beans, potatoes, green beans, onion, garlic, tapioca, curry powder, coriander, red pepper (if desired), salt, and cinnamon. Pour broth over all. Cover; cook on low-heat setting for 8 to 10 hours or on high-heat setting for 4 to 5 hours. Stir in Undrained tomatoes. Cover; let stand 5 minutes.

Serve with cooked rice. Makes 4 servings.

VEGETABLE PASTA FOR CROCKPOT
* 2 tablespoons Butter Or Margarine
* 1 Zucchini, 1/4" slice
* 1 Yellow Squash, 1/4" slice
* 2 Carrots, thinly sliced
* 1 1/2 cups Mushrooms, fresh, sliced
* 1 package Broccoli, Frozen, cuts
* 4 Green Onions, sliced
* 2 to 3 cloves Garlic, minced
* 1/2 teaspoon Basil, dried
* 1/4 teaspoon Salt
* 1/2 teaspoon Pepper
* 1 cup Parmesan Cheese, grated
* 12 ounces Fettucine
* 1 cup Mozzarella Cheese,
* Shredded
* 1 cup Cream
* 2 Egg Yolks

Rub crock wall with butter. Put zucchini, yellow squash, carrots, mushrooms, broccoli, onions, garlic, seasonings and parmesan in the Crock Pot. Cover; cook on High 2 hours. Cook fettucine according to package directions; drain. Add cooked fettucine, mozzarella, cream and egg yolks. Stir to blend well. Allow to heat for 15 to 30 minutes. For serving turn to Low for up to 30 minutes.

Serves 6.

VEGETABLE SLOW COOKER
8 Potatoes
1 Onion, chopped
4 Carrots, peeled and sliced
2 Stalks celery, sliced
4 Chicken bouillon cubes
1 tablespoon Parsley flakes
5 cups Water
1/3 cup Butter or margarine
Ham - cubed to taste
13 ounces Can evaporated milk

Peel & cut potatoes into bite-sized pieces. Put all ingredients except evaporated milk in Crock Pot. Cover and cook 10 to 12 hours. Stir in evaporated milk during last hour. Add flour to thicken, if desired. This is made in the Crock Pot-very easy recipes and yummy!

VEGETABLES ITALIAN-STYLE
1 teaspoon salt
1 medium eggplant, cut in 1" cubes
2 to 3 medium zucchini, halved & sliced 1/2"
1 large onion, sliced thinly
12 ounces fresh mushrooms, sliced
1 tablespoon olive oil
4 plum tomatoes, sliced 1/4" thick
1 1/2 cups mozzarella cheese, shredded
2 cups tomato sauce
1 teaspoon oregano
salt and pepper, to taste

Toss eggplant and zucchini with the 1 teaspoon of salt. Place in a large colander over a bowl to drain for about 1 hour. Drain and squeeze excess moisture out. In a large skillet over medium heat, saute onion, eggplant, zucchini, and mushrooms until slightly tender. In the slow cooker/Crock Pot, layer 1/3 of the vegetables (including sliced tomatoes), 1/3 of the the tomato sauce. and 1/3 of the cheese. Sprinkle with oregano, salt and pepper. Repeat layering 2 more times.

Cover and cook on low 6 to 8 hours. Serve over rice, pasta, or other grain.

    Serves 6.

VELVEETA SALSA DIP
    * 1 pound Velveeta Cheese spread, cubed (can use light
    * 1 package Picante sauce or salsa
    * 2 tablespoons Cilantro (optional)
    1. Place brick of Velveeta and jar of picante sauce in a slow cooker or Crock Pot, and turn on high stirring occasionally until melted and blended. Stir in cilantro when melted.
    2. Serve with tortilla chips.
    Note: You can substitute two cans of chopped tomatoes and chiles for the salsa, or add one can of tomatoes and chiles. Play around with this, and you might even add a little Louisiana hot sauce!

White Chili with Chicken
    1 lb. dry white northern beans
    5 1/4 c. chicken broth
    2 cloves garlic, minced
    1 lg. white onion, chopped
    1 tbsp. ground white pepper
    1 tsp. salt
    1 tbsp. dried oregano
    1 tbsp. ground cumin
    1/2 tsp. ground cloves
    1 (7 oz.) can diced green chilies
    5 c. diced cooked chicken breast
    1 3/4 c. chicken broth
    1 tbsp. diced jalapeno pepper
    (optional)
    Flour tortillas
    Condiments:
    Shredded Monterey Jack cheese
    Sliced black olives
    Chunky salsa
    Sour cream
    Diced avocados

Soak beans in water to cover for 24 hours then drain. In slow cooker/Crock Pot or large kettle, combine beans, 5 1/4 cup chicken broth, garlic, onion, white pepper, salt, oregano, cumin, cloves. Simmer covered for at least 5 hours until beans are tender. Stir occasionally. Stir in green chiles, chicken and 1 3/4 chicken broth. For hotter taste, add jalapeno. Cover and simmer for 1 hour. Serve with flour tortillas and condiments.

WILD RICE CASSEROLE
1 1/2 c. uncooked long-grained rice
1/2 c. uncooked wild rice
1 envelope dry onion soup mix
1 tbsp. snipped parsley (optional)
4 c. water
1 bunch green onions, chopped
8 oz. fresh or canned mushrooms, sliced
1/4 c. butter or margarine, melted
Combine all ingredients. Pour into lightly greased slow cooker. Cover, cook on high 2 1/2 hours, stirring occasionally.

WINNING WINGS IN SWEET AND SOUR SAUCE
* 16 Chicken wings
* 4 tablespoons Wine or balsamic vinegar
* 1 cup Apricot preserves
* 2 tablespoons Peanut butter (optional)
* 1 cup Ketchup
* 4 tablespoons Horseradish
* 1 cup Sweet onion, finely chopped
* 1 teaspoon Hot sauce (optional)
Pat the chicken wings dry and place them in the slow cooker/Crock Pot.

In a bowl, mix together remaining ingredients.

Taste-check for a good balance of sweet and sour.

Pour the sauce over the wings. Cover the slow cooker/Crock Pot and cook on low until the chicken is tender, about 4 hours.

YUMMY CHICKEN WINGS
12-18 chicken wings

1/3 c soy sauce
1 tsp. ginger
2 garlic cloves minced
2 green onions minced
1 TBS honey
2 tsp. oil
Combine ingredients in your Crock Pot!! Cook on low for 6-8 hours serves 2-4 people depending on appetizer or main dish

ZUCCHINI BREAD

* 2 eggs
* 2/3 c. vegetable oil
* 1 1/4 cup sugar
* 1 1/3 c. zucchini, peeled and grated
* 2 tsp. vanilla
* 2 c. flour
* 1/4 tsp. salt
* 1/2 tsp. baking powder
* 1 tsp. cinnamon
* 1/2 tsp. nutmeg
* 1/2 to 1 c. chopped nuts

With mixer, beat eggs until light and foamy. Add oil, sugar, grated zucchini and vanilla. Mix well. Stir dry ingredients with nuts. Add to zucchini mixture. Mix well. Pour into greased and floured 2 pound coffee can or 2 quart mold. Place in Crock Pot. Cover top with 8 paper towels. Cover and bake on high 3 to 4 hours. DO NOT CHECK OR REMOVE cover until last hour of baking. Let stand 5 minutes before unmolding.

ZUCCHINI CASSEROLE

1 red onion, sliced
1 green pepper, cut in thin strips
4 med. zucchini, sliced & unpeeled
1 (16 oz.) can diced tomatoes, undrained
1 tsp. salt
1/2 tsp. pepper
1/2 tsp. basil
1 tbsp. oleo

1/4 c. grated Parmesan cheese

Combine all ingredients, except oleo and cheese, in a slow cooker. Set temperature on low and heat for 3 hours. Dot casserole with oleo and sprinkle with cheese. Cook 1 1/2 hours more on low setting.

Makes 6 servings.

4419907

Made in the USA
Lexington, KY
23 January 2010